Wisdom Across Generations

"Conversations with My Great-Grandchildren"

Fiction or Fact ?

By

M.N.Ashraf

Table of Contents

Foreword

Dear Grandpa,

We've asked you so many questions as your great-grandchildren —
Big ones. Brave ones.
About life and death.
About love, time, fear, and God.
About war and peace…
And what truly matters when we grow up.

You didn't answer like a teacher.
You answered like a grandfather—
With stories that made us laugh,
With silences that made us think,
And sometimes, with quiet tears that spoke louder than any words.

You listened to our small voices as if they were the most important in the world.
You made us feel that every question—no matter how simple—was full of meaning.
This book is full of those precious conversations.
Full of wonder, truth, dreams, and love.
And maybe... just a little bit of magic too.

We hope children and grandparents everywhere read this—
From the sunlit streets of Riyadh and Sana'a,
To the quiet corners of Gaza,
From playgrounds in New York, London, and Munich,
To rooftops in Pyongyang, Beijing, and beyond.

To every reader, young or old,
Our message is simple, but strong:
We want one thing, and one thing only—peace. For everyone.
Everywhere. Forever.
So that every child may smile freely,

Every mother may sleep peacefully,
Every bird may leave its nest, knowing its chicks are safe,
And every lioness may go in search of food, trusting her cubs are unharmed in their den.

We are proud to be part of this book.
But even prouder to be your grandchildren.

With all our love,
Mariyam, Ibrahim & Yousuf

Foreword

The author and I share a bond that goes back over 55 years—friends, classmates, and fellow engineers from the same college. What began in our youthful days of learning has grown into a lifelong friendship rooted in mutual respect and admiration. Over the decades, I've seen him evolve—not just as a brilliant Mechanical Engineer with vast field experience in gas turbines and power plant engineering, but also as a man of deep wisdom, humility, and integrity.

In recent years, post-retirement, he surprised many of us by unlocking a remarkable new talent—writing. But knowing him, I wasn't surprised by the depth and clarity he brought to his books. He's never done anything halfway. His works, including *A Handbook on Gas Turbines*, *Sands of Time* (his touching memoir of 39 years in Saudi Arabia), and *Sunset to Sunrise* (a practical guide to retirement), are a reflection of the same excellence and sincerity that defined his engineering career.

Now, with *Conversations with My Great-Grandchildren – Fiction or Fact?*, he turns his attention to one of the most pressing and timeless themes—bridging generations. In today's rapidly changing world, where technology connects us but emotions often divide us, this book offers a fresh, heartfelt perspective. Through the lens of tender yet thoughtful conversations with his great-grandchildren, he explores the widening generational gap—with warmth, humor, empathy, and insight.

I've had the pleasure of reading several excerpts and previews he shared with me during the writing process. I was deeply impressed—not just by the content, but by the sincerity of his purpose. This is not just a book—it's a message to global society. A reminder that wisdom is not confined to age, and understanding is not bound by time.

In these pages, you'll find not just reflections, but bridges—between the past and the present, between logic and emotion, between generations who often talk *past* each other rather than *to* each other.

I consider this work a gift—not just from a friend, but from a wise elder to the world. I wish him great success and hope this book reaches the hearts of readers young and old.

Sincerely,
Sushil Sharma

Preface

The boundless curiosity of my grandchildren has been the spark that ignited the creation of this book. Their generation, thriving in the marvels of modern technology, continually amazes me with their effortless grasp of computers, fascination with space exploration, and wonder at the mysteries of galaxies and oceans. They dream of a future shaped by groundbreaking developments in artificial intelligence and robotics—a world where robots perform all types of jobs with precision, from diagnosing and treating cancer to conducting heart transplants and even brain surgeries. They envision unmanned missions venturing to Mars and beyond our galaxy, unraveling the secrets of the cosmos.

Each conversation with them feels like a thrilling journey into this incredible future, where their probing questions and insatiable thirst for knowledge challenge me to keep learning and growing. Through their eyes, I've rediscovered the joy of exploring life's mysteries and marveled at the limitless potential of human ingenuity. This book is a testament to that shared adventure, celebrating the boundless imagination and aspirations that drive us toward a better tomorrow.

It was during these engaging conversations that a spark ignited within me—a thought to write a book capturing the dynamic exchanges between generations. Why limit this to two generations, though? Why not stretch the dialogue across a three-generational gap, involving great-grandfather and great-grandchildren? This idea intrigued me. The sheer breadth of such a conversation, spanning nearly a century, could serve as a fascinating framework to weave fiction with facts. It opened a fascinating gateway for me to explore the ever-evolving realms of technology, science, politics, and the economy—unraveling the rise of Artificial Intelligence, the expanding frontiers of the cosmos, and the enduring mystery of creation.

But beyond these advancements, I saw a deeper conversation waiting to unfold—the shifting values of humanity itself. The pursuit of money and materialism has increasingly shaped our world, often blurring the true essence of a peaceful life. Have we, in our relentless race for wealth and possessions, lost sight of the real purpose of life? Would my great-grandchildren, growing up in an era of hyper-connectivity and digital dominance, view happiness differently than I did? Through this book, I wished to explore not just progress but also the wisdom passed down through generations—on contentment, simplicity, and the balance between ambition and inner peace.

Imagine a world where humanity's understanding of reality has undergone profound transformations—from believing in a flat Earth to recognizing our planet as a magnificent sphere and now an oblate spheroid, from marveling at the moon's radiant glow to discovering its simple sunlight reflected off its surface. These once-revolutionary insights now seem almost ordinary, yet they remind us of the boundless journey of human curiosity and discovery.

Today, we stand in awe of an expanding universe, where the mysteries of light and rays from distant galaxies hold the keys to cosmic secrets. These ancient travelers, who have crossed billions of years, carry stories of their origins, whispering truths about their composition, distance, and the forces that shaped them. They are like time capsules, offering glimpses into the very fabric of creation.

Equally inspiring are our achievements closer to home. We celebrate milestones like unmanned spacecraft exploring Mars, mapping its red sands, and revealing its secrets. And who can resist imagining what lies ahead? Will humanity establish settlements on the Moon or Mars, turning science fiction into fact—just as Isaac Asimov, Arthur C. Clarke, and Robert Heinlein once envisioned in their legendary works? Could the enigma of flying saucers and alien life—long the subject of wonder—finally be unveiled, shifting the boundaries of what we know about life beyond Earth, much like the stories that once fueled our imagination?

As we ponder these possibilities, we realize that each revelation brings us closer to understanding the cosmos and ourselves—our capacity for exploration, imagination, and connection to the infinite. What extraordinary chapters lie ahead in this grand story of discovery? Only time will tell.

Between the birth of Artificial Intelligence and its evolving role in tackling global issues lies a fascinating journey—a glimpse into a future where solutions might emerge without the complexities of human involvement or interference. It's both thrilling and unsettling to imagine a world reshaped by AI's vast capabilities.

I must admit, the thought of such profound changes stirs a whirlwind of excitement and apprehension within me. What will it mean for humanity when decisions no longer rely on the depth of human intuition or the warmth of emotion? Will we be stepping into an era of flawless precision, or will we unknowingly walk into a labyrinth of unforeseen challenges?

It is hardly surprising that the future may render traditional courts and judges obsolete—no longer swayed by limited knowledge, outdated interpretations, or the pressures of political influence. Instead, Artificial Intelligence may take the reins of justice, delivering verdicts rooted in pure logic and untainted fairness. With no room for bias, emotion, or external pressure, will AI finally achieve what humans never could—a system of judgment that is truly just, leaving no space for doubt? Or will the absence of human conscience in justice lead us into an ethical void we have yet to comprehend?

For now, I've decided to embrace this book as a delightful work of fiction—a playful journey through ideas that could, one day, take root in reality. Who knows? The future has a way of surprising us! So, let's keep the spirit of hope alive, immerse ourselves in these lively conversations, and revel in the curiosity, wonder, and imagination that breathe life into every page. Read with an open heart, let your imagination soar, and dare to dream of the possibilities waiting beyond the horizon.

This book delves into these gaps of knowledge, blending the past, present, and future through conversations that traverse time. It poses a fascinating question: How would a great-grandfather, shaped by the values and limitations of his era, respond to the futuristic questions of a tech-savvy great-grandchild? The answers remain an exciting mystery waiting to unfold.

I invite you to embark on this journey with me—a journey through time, imagination, and intellect. Each page is crafted to ignite your curiosity, challenge your perspectives, and enrich your understanding of our ever-evolving world. Whether it's the playful banter or the profound reflections, I hope this book captivates your mind and heart.

Thank you for joining me in this exploration. I sincerely hope it brings you as much joy in reading as it brought me in writing. Let's dive into this fictional yet thought-provoking world together and make the most of every moment we share.

Finally, my deepest thanks go to the three stars of this book—Mariyam, Ibrahim, and Yousuf—whose innocent curiosity became the driving force behind every page. You didn't just ask questions; you asked the right ones—tough, thoughtful, and profoundly genuine. Through your eyes, the forgotten truths of our world came alive again. Your voices gave this book its soul. Thank you for reminding me, and hopefully the readers, of what truly matters on this planet we all share.

I also cannot forget the loving circle that made the completion of this book possible.

To my beloved wife, Monawar—your quiet strength and unwavering moral support carried me through the toughest moments.

To my sons, Nadeem and Naseem—thank you for your constant encouragement, your technical guidance, and your wholehearted help during the publication process.

To my daughter, Dr. Nahid, your belief in this project gave me the emotional momentum I often needed.

To my wonderful daughter-in-law, Engineer Sharmeen, and my caring son-in-law, Dr. Fahad—your kindness, your thoughtful gestures, and your encouragement meant more to me than words can express.

From the depths of my heart, I offer my sincere gratitude and warmest thanks to each of you. This book carries pieces of all of you within its pages.

Last, but by no means least, my heartfelt gratitude goes to my dear colleagues — Bhunesh Mathur, Ashok Ahluwalia, Sushil Sharma, A.K. Banik, and R.B. Mathur — whose unwavering support, thoughtful guidance, and deep reservoirs of wisdom and experience were a constant source of strength for me.

Throughout this journey, I shared many excerpts of this book with them — not just for feedback, but to make them a part of this creation, as they rightfully deserve to be. Their sincere encouragement and invaluable advice often lit the path ahead when I stumbled in doubt or hesitation.

To each of you — thank you, from the depths of my heart. This book carries your fingerprints in its pages, and your kindness in its soul.

Disclaimer: This book is a work of fiction. All names, characters, places, and events are products of the author's imagination or are used fictitiously. Any resemblance to actual persons, living or dead, or real locations is purely coincidental.The author does not intend to target, criticize, or offend any individual or group, nor to diminish anyone's dignity through these conversations. Instead, the purpose of this work is to inspire thought, reflection, and meaningful discussion, without bias or personal judgment. In a world often marked by tension and unrest, this book seeks to offer a touch of humor and introspection, aiming to bring a sense of calm and contemplation to its readers.

Happy reading

M.N. Ashraf

Introduction

Wisdom Across Generations

Conversations with My Great-Grandchildren – Fiction or Fact?

Imagine a world where the boundless curiosity of youth meets the profound wisdom of age, creating a bridge that spans nearly a century of experiences. This book is a whimsical journey into such a world, where the great-grandchildren's questions form the backbone of a delightful future exploration. Yet, the answers remain hidden here, waiting to unfold in the detailed chapters ahead, where Great Grandpa will weave them with wisdom, humor, and the occasional playful dodge.

This is not just a book but an invitation to dream, laugh, and ponder. Through the playful, curious, and sometimes downright hilarious questions of great-grandchildren, we explore a kaleidoscope of ideas. From futuristic trains soaring across oceans to robots negotiating peace treaties, every question is a doorway to a world of imagination and wonder.

There are questions—deep, haunting, and filled with raw emotion. The great-grandchildren, their voices trembling, paint vivid pictures of today's technological marvels and the shadows they cast. Their innocent hearts, burdened by the weight of a world in turmoil, cannot hold back their tears. And neither can Great Grandpa. Together, they grieve for the uncertain future unfolding before them.

But within those tears lies wisdom—hard-earned, timeless, and unshaken. Answers that do not dismiss their fears but illuminate them. Truths that challenge, comfort, and inspire.

To witness this heartfelt exchange—of questions that pierce the soul and responses that carry the weight of generations—dive into this book. Listen to the concerns of young minds grappling with a world on the edge, and perhaps, find your answers along the way.

The Unanswered Questions That Sparked a Journey

- **Futuristic Travel:**
  - "Great Grandpa, what would it be like to soar across the Atlantic and Pacific Oceans in supersonic trains, faster than sound, just like space stations? Would they brave storms, float amid raging seas, and pass unscathed through the Bermuda Triangle?"
- **Robots in Power:**
  - "Do you think robots will one day represent countries at G20 summits? Will they negotiate without bias or emotion or fall into corruption like some politicians today?"
- **War and Peace:**
  - "Great Grandpa, why do powerful nations keep waging wars, causing suffering and genocide? When will leaders trade power for peace and selfish ambition for shared prosperity? Could wars fought by robots bring even greater destruction than humans?"
- **The Threat of World War III:**
  - "Einstein said that World War IV would be fought with sticks and stones. Does that mean World War III will destroy everything? Is there hope for a future of peace, love, and dreams?"
- **AI and Healthcare:**
  - "Will we need doctors in the future, or will robots cure cancer, transplant hearts, and even replant brains? Can AI create vaccines for diseases like cancer, just like humans for COVID-19?"
- **Robots at Home:**
  - "Will robots serve us tea, remind us to take medicines, and replace servants stuck in traffic? Will they make life easier for everyone?"
- **AI-Driven Governance:**

    - “Could robots in parliament stop the production of weapons of mass destruction? Could they solve inflation, unemployment, and the widening gap between rich and poor?”
- **Space Exploration:**
    - “Do you think we’ll colonize the Moon, Mars, or planets beyond our solar system? Will we find alien life? Could Elon Musk be right about humans inhabiting Mars?”
- **The Mystery of Creation:**
    - "Will AI or even humanity itself—ever unlock the deepest secrets of creation? Are we truly on the brink of grasping the essence of life, or are we merely wandering through the endless corridors of mystery? If we succeed, will the future shine with the brilliance and beauty we dream of, or will we unveil truths so profound that they redefine our very existence?
    - As we push the boundaries of knowledge, are we awakening to a grand design or daring to rewrite the story of creation itself?"
- **Understanding Diseases and Their Impact on Life:**
    - In today’s fast-paced world, how is mental and emotional health being affected?.
    - What lessons can we learn from past pandemics, and how can we protect ourselves in an ever-changing world?
    - could ancient wisdom and traditional healing practices still hold the key to longevity and well-being?

Why This Book Matters

In an era of rapid technological advancements, humanity finds itself at a crossroads. Artificial Intelligence reshapes the way we think and live, while generational gaps deepen the divide between tech-savvy youth and bewildered elders. This book attempts to bridge that divide, using fictional dialogues inspired by real-life questions to explore the evolving relationships between generations.

Through the lens of fiction, the **great-grandchildren**'s questions explore societal dilemmas, technological marvels, and humanity's timeless challenges. Each question invites the reader to imagine, laugh, and reflect on the possibilities of the future.

A Journey Through Generations

While the **great-grandchildren**'s questions remain unanswered in this introduction, the detailed chapters promise to reveal the **great-grandfather**'s wisdom, forged from decades of experience. These conversations are more than words—they are bridges of understanding, illuminating the bond between knowledge and imagination.

So, let's embark on this journey together. Let's dive into these conversations, dream big, and explore what the future might hold. Read this book with an open heart and mind, and who knows—you might just find yourself inspired to ask your **great-grandchild** a question one day.

As you turn the pages, let curiosity guide you. Ask yourself: Are these questions mere flights of fancy, or are they glimpses into a world yet to come? Dive into this intergenerational adventure and decide for yourself: **is it fiction, fact, or a little of both?**

Session One

Wisdom Across Generations

Introducing Legendary Great Grandpa

The spring morning was nothing short of magical. The mellow, golden sun filtered gently through the netted curtains, casting playful patterns on the wooden floor. Outside, a harmonious blend of warmth and a crisp, cool breeze carried the delicate fragrance of blooming flowers into the family room, setting the perfect stage for an unforgettable reunion.

In the heart of this serene setting sat **Great Grandpa**—a majestic figure whose very presence encapsulated the magic of the day. Born and raised in British India, he had journeyed to Monte Lindo Ct in San Jose, California, to spend precious moments with his great-grandchildren. At 99 years old, he radiated wisdom and vitality, his white beard framing a face etched with the profound stories of a century gone by. Draped in a striking red-and-white gown that lent him an air of regal charm, he reclined in his favorite armchair, cradling a steaming cup of morning coffee. The rich aroma mingled with the freshness of spring, evoking a timeless dance between past and present.

The soft sound of footsteps descending the stairs broke the gentle stillness. **Mariyam**, **Ibrahim**, and **Yousuf**—his beloved great-grandchildren—emerged from their bedrooms, their sleepy faces lighting up at the sight of him. "Good morning, **Great Grandpa**!" they chorused, their voices bubbling with love and cheer.

Great Grandpa's heart swelled with joy. "Ah, my little angels!" he exclaimed, spreading his arms wide in welcome. His voice, though touched by time, enveloped the children like a cozy, familiar blanket. **Yousuf**, the youngest, darted forward, climbing onto his lap with a burst of giggles, snuggling close as if to capture every word of his wisdom. **Maryam**, the eldest, settled comfortably on the sofa to his right, while

Ibrahim perched on the left, his eyes wide with anticipation. Amid the morning chatter, **Great Grandpa** gently inquired about their well-being. They reassured him with tales of peaceful sleep and a few humorous incidents, like the occasional fox cry outside that had momentarily startled them.

After a thoughtful sip of his steaming coffee, **Great Grandpa's** eyes twinkled as he posed a question that had long lingered in his heart: "Do you know the story of our family? Do you know the legacy and rich history behind us?" The children's responses were a chorus of innocence and curiosity, "No, **Great Grandpa**, tell us everything! We want to know all about our family's past and your remarkable life. And one day, we'll throw you the grandest birthday party for your 100th birthday!"

A smile danced on his lips as he began his tale—a journey that spanned continents, wars, and the evolution of a nation. "I was born in a remote village in British India, in a time when the world was vastly different from today. In our tiny village, there were no roads, no electricity, no telephone, no water supply, and not even a proper school or hospital. Life was simple yet profound. My parents were landlords who owned vast farmlands, while many of our neighbors toiled as laborers in the fields. Those were days when radio was the window to the world—television, telephones, and modern gadgets were things of the future. We rose with the sun and rested as it set, our lives marked by the rhythm of nature."

He continued, his voice rich with nostalgia and pride, "My grandparents adored me, for I was the only son in our family. They spared no effort in nurturing my education. A dedicated tutor taught me languages—Urdu, Hindi, English, Persian, and Arabic—as well as the fundamentals of arithmetic. At the age of twelve, I was sent to a nearby district town, some 20 miles away, for formal schooling. There, servants cared for me, and every meal was prepared fresh and organically, without the adulteration or preservatives that are common today."

Great Grandpa's eyes sparkled as he recounted the era of his youth, "When World War II erupted in September 1939, the world was plunged into chaos. Germany, under Hitler's tyranny, had already cast a dark shadow over Europe, and millions were caught in the tempest of war. There was a tremendous demand for soldiers, and my academic achievements, combined with my family background, opened a path for me in the British Indian Army. I was recruited as a foot soldier and soon found myself deployed in Italy, a land as rich in history as it was in the scars of war. The battles were fierce, and the spirit of camaraderie among soldiers, regardless of nationality, was something I cherished deeply. I served with honor until the war's end in September 1945."

He paused, allowing the weight of history to settle before continuing, "But even as I served, the fight for freedom back home was growing stronger. The Indian independence movement, which had simmered since 1857, gathered immense momentum during those turbulent times. Upon returning to India, I resigned from the Army and joined the struggle for freedom, inspired by the non-violent resistance championed by Mahatma Gandhi. It was a defining chapter in our nation's history—a battle not fought with weapons, but with unwavering determination and peaceful resolve. When India finally won its independence on August 15, 1947, a new era dawned."

Great Grandpa's voice softened as he reflected on his journey, "After the war, I was offered several government and private positions, but my heart was set on building a future for my family. I moved to Patna, India, where opportunities flourished, and dedicated myself to nurturing the next generation through education and love."

As he wove these memories, the room filled with a palpable sense of wonder and reverence. The great-grandchildren listened, enraptured, their imaginations ignited by visions of dusty Indian villages, the thunder of wartime battles, and the fervor of a nation fighting for its soul. Every detail of his narration painted a vivid tapestry of a past that was both distant and deeply personal.

The story of **Great Grandpa** was more than a recounting of historical events; it was a living legacy—a bridge connecting the simplicity of early life in a remote village to the complexities of a modern, vibrant world. His journey from the rustic lanes of British India to the bustling streets of San Jose, California was a testament to resilience, courage, and the enduring power of family bonds.

In that luminous spring morning, as the fragrant air mingled with timeless memories, Great Grandpa's tales illuminated not just the history of a nation, but the very soul of a family. His legacy was a beacon, guiding his great-grandchildren to understand that every chapter of their past—filled with struggles, triumphs, and dreams—was a vital part of the remarkable story that was their heritage.

At the end of a long journey through the memories of his life, the **great-grandchildren** leaned forward, eyes sparkling with curiosity, and asked, "**Great Grandpa**, what was your role in Italy during the Second World War?" A knowing smile lit up his weathered face as he set down his steaming cup of coffee, ready to transport them to a time of courage, camaraderie, and the surreal beauty of a war-torn land.

Maryam, her eyes gleaming with curiosity, unleashed a barrage of questions, eager to unravel the untold tales of **Great Grandpa**'s time in the British Indian Army during World War II in Italy. With a nostalgic smile, **Great Grandpa** leaned back, ready to dust off memories buried in the trenches of time. The stories were about to begin…

Maryam, *fired the first of her many questions, setting the stage for a journey back in time: "**Great Grandpa**, how and when did you join the British Indian Army?"*

Great Grandpa: Oh, my dear **Maryam**, that's a story worth telling! It was 1942, and thc world was in chaos. I was a young lad, full of energy and curiosity, though not particularly fond of waking up early—something the army quickly fixed! They needed strong, brave young men to serve, and before I knew it, I was marching in a uniform that was two sizes too big for me. The recruiting officer looked at me and said, "You have good eyesight, strong legs, and—most importantly—you seem too naïve to say no!" And that's how I ended up in the British Indian Army.

Maryam: Great Grandpa - *Could you please give us a captivating glimpse into the heroic battles fought by the British Indian Army in Italy during World War II?*

Greta Grandpa: During World War II, the British Indian Army played a crucial role in the Italian Campaign (1943–1945), fighting with immense bravery and resilience against the Axis forces. Over 50000 Indian soldiers were part of the British Indian Army, making it the largest volunteer force in history.

In Italy, Indian troops fought in some of the most grueling battles, including the Battle of Monte Cassino and the Gothic Line offensive. Facing treacherous mountain terrain, extreme weather, and fierce German resistance, they showcased remarkable courage and determination.

The 4th, 8th, and 10th Indian Divisions were instrumental in breaking through enemy defenses, capturing key positions, and supporting Allied advances. Their contributions helped secure victories that eventually led to the fall of fascist Italy.

Despite their sacrifices, the stories of these unsung heroes remain largely overshadowed. Thousands of Indian soldiers were wounded or lost their lives, earning gallantry awards such as the Victoria Cross. Their legacy stands as a testament to the bravery, discipline, and unwavering commitment of the British Indian Army during WWII.

Maryam: *What was your rank and role during the war?*

Great Grandpa: Ah, rank and role! Now that's a tricky one. I started as a simple foot soldier followed by promotions in officer rank, which meant I was excellent at following orders and even better at running when bullets started flying. But soon, my officers realized I had a knack for mechanics—probably because I had spent my childhood fixing broken bicycles in the village. So, they assigned me to maintain and repair military vehicles. You could say I became a 'Doctor for Jeeps and Trucks.' No medals for fixing a truck, but believe me, if that truck didn't work, neither did the soldiers!

Maryam: *Were you assigned to a specific regiment or division?*

Great Grandpa: Oh yes! I was part of an engineering and logistics division. We weren't the ones charging with bayonets, but let me tell you, without us, those bayonets wouldn't reach the battlefield. We ensured supplies, ammunition, and vehicles were in top condition. You could call us the 'Backstage Heroes.' Our motto? "If it moves, we fix it. If it doesn't, we push it!"

Maryam: *How did you feel when you were informed about your posting in Italy?*

Great Grandpa: Ah, Italy! When they told me, I thought, "Finally! A place famous for pizza and beautiful scenery!" But, my dear, reality was far from that. Instead of sightseeing in Rome, I was knee-deep in mud, dodging bombs, and trying to repair vehicles under enemy fire. My excitement quickly turned into, "I hope I get to eat a proper meal before the next air raid!" But I must admit, the Italians were warm-hearted people, and their food—when we managed to get some—was a welcome break from the army rations.

Maryam: *What kind of training did you receive before being sent to war?*

Great Grandpa: Oh, training? You mean the art of waking up before sunrise, running until your legs give up, and learning how to shout "Yes, Sir!" louder than your own thoughts? Yes, I had plenty of that! We were trained to march, shoot, crawl through mud, and repair vehicles in the worst conditions. One of my sergeants used to say, "If you can fix a truck while being shot at, congratulations—you're ready!" It was tough, but in hindsight, it taught me discipline, endurance, and the ability to sleep anywhere—even on a moving truck!

Maryam: *Wow, **Great Grandpa**, you've had quite an adventure!*

Great Grandpa: Adventure? Ha! My dear, an adventure is when you go looking for fun. This was more like being thrown into a wild storm without an umbrella. But looking back, it made me who I am today. And now, I get to tell you these stories while sitting in a comfortable chair with a cup of coffee—something I never took for granted after the war!

Maryam's Inquiry into Great-Grandpa's Wartime Journey

Maryam *(leaning forward with curiosity):* ***Great-Grandpa****, you mentioned that you were sent to fight in Italy during World War II. That's so far away from India! How did you even get there?*

Great-Grandpa (smiling at her eager face): Ah, my dear **Maryam**, it was a long and exhausting journey. We boarded a troopship from Bombay (now Mumbai), packed like sardines with hundreds of other soldiers. The ship sailed through the Arabian Sea, passed through the Suez Canal in Egypt, and into the Mediterranean Sea. The voyage took several weeks, and the conditions were tough—rough seas, extreme heat during the day, and bone-chilling cold at night.

Maryam (wide-eyed): *That sounds terrifying! What did you do all those weeks on the ship?*

Great-Grandpa (chuckling): We passed the time with drills, exercises, and endless stories about home. Some of us played cards, while others just stared at the endless ocean, wondering what lay ahead. But deep down, we all had the same thought—will we survive this war and return home?

Maryam (softly): *That must have been scary... And when you finally reached Italy, what were your first impressions?*

Great-Grandpa (pausing, lost in memory): When we landed in Italy, I was struck by how beautiful yet war-torn it was. The rolling hills, the ancient buildings... but many had been reduced to rubble. The air smelled of gunpowder, and the roads were filled with military convoys and destroyed vehicles. Civilians looked at us with a mixture of hope and fear—hope that we would drive the enemy away, and fear that the war would never end.

Maryam (thoughtful): *That must have been overwhelming. Where exactly in Italy were you stationed?*

Great-Grandpa (nodding): My battalion was deployed near Monte Cassino, one of the toughest battlegrounds of the war. It was a strategic point heavily defended by the Germans. The fighting was brutal—rain, mud, and constant shelling. But we knew that if we captured that area, we could open the way for the Allied forces to push further north.

Maryam (in awe): *Monte Cassino? I read about that in history! You were really in the middle of one of the biggest battles?*

Great-Grandpa (smiling with pride): Yes, my child. And let me tell you, history books can't capture what it truly felt like to be there...

Then came Ibrahim, intelligently waiting for his turn in order to ask series of questions of his test to his great grandpa

The Ibrahim's Relentless Curiosity and Great-Grandpa's War Stories

Great-Grandpa had just earned "full marks" from Ibrahim's quiz, but the young boy was not done yet. His thirst for knowledge—and perhaps a little mischief—made him press forward with more questions. He leaned in, adjusting his imaginary military cap, ready to fire off another round of queries.

Ibrahim (grinning): *Alright, Great-Grandpa, you may have passed the first round, but I still have more questions!*

Great-Grandpa (chuckling): Oh, so this isn't over yet? Fine, young commander, let's see what else you've got!

The Harsh Reality of War – Weather & Terrain

Ibrahim: *What was the weather and terrain like in Italy? And how did it affect combat?*

Great-Grandpa (his face turning serious): The terrain was brutal, my boy. Italy is full of mountains, rivers, and dense forests. The roads were narrow and muddy, making it nearly impossible for tanks to move. The Germans had the high ground, which meant we had to climb steep hills under heavy fire.

And the weather? *Ahh!* In winter, the cold was merciless. Our boots would freeze, and our hands would go numb holding our rifles. In the rainy season, the entire battlefield turned into a swamp of mud, making every step exhausting. Many soldiers fell sick before even reaching the enemy.

Ibrahim (wide-eyed): *That sounds horrible! So what kind of weapons did you have to fight in such conditions?*

Great-Grandpa (nodding): We carried Lee-Enfield rifles, which were good but required manual reloading after every shot. Some of us had Bren light machine guns, which were excellent for covering fire. The British forces provided grenades, bayonets, and mortars, but compared to the German firepower, we often felt under-equipped. They had MG-42 machine guns—deadly weapons that could fire hundreds of bullets in seconds!

Maryam (nervously): *And you had to fight against that?*

Great-Grandpa (sighing): Yes, my dear. And it wasn't just about bullets—it was about strategy, survival, and sheer willpower.

Battle & War Front Experience

Ibrahim's *curiosity burned brighter. He wanted to know more—much more.*

Ibrahim: *Which battles did you fight in while in Italy?*

Great-Grandpa: The most brutal one was Monte Cassino, where we fought for months to break through the German defenses. I also took part in the battles around Anzio and Florence, where the fighting was intense, and every inch of land was soaked in blood.

Ibrahim (leaning forward): *Did you ever directly fight against German or Italian forces?*

Great-Grandpa (nodding slowly): Yes. In Monte Cassino, we faced elite German paratroopers and Panzer divisions. They were highly trained and well-armed. Many times, it was close combat—bayonets, grenades, and hand-to-hand fights in the trenches.

Ibrahim (in awe): *That must have been terrifying… How did British Indian soldiers coordinate with the other Allied forces?*

Great-Grandpa: It wasn't always easy. We had soldiers from Britain, America, Canada, Poland, and even New Zealand fighting together. Communication was a challenge due to different languages, but we all had the same goal—to push back the Axis forces. Sometimes, our officers would give orders in English, which many Indian soldiers struggled to understand, but we relied on each other and made it work. For me English was not the language barrier.

The Hardships of War

Ibrahim (growing serious): *What was the hardest challenge you faced on the battlefield?*

Great-Grandpa took a deep breath, his fingers gently tapping the armrest of his chair.

Great-Grandpa: Losing my comrades. You can prepare for bullets and bombs, but nothing prepares you for the sight of your friends falling beside you. The sound of a dying soldier calling for his mother in his final moments... *that stays with you forever.*

Maryam and Ibrahim exchanged glances. The room felt heavier now.

Ibrahim (softly): *Were you ever injured?*

Great-Grandpa (rolling up his sleeve, revealing an old scar on his arm): A bullet grazed me during a night raid near Florence. I was lucky. Many others weren't.

Maryam (whispering): *I can't imagine what that must have been like...*

Life as a Soldier

Ibrahim decided to lighten the mood.

Ibrahim (trying to smile): *Okay, Great-Grandpa, let's talk about something less scary. What was daily life like in the army?*

Great-Grandpa (chuckling again): Ha! *Daily life?* If you call waking up at dawn, marching for miles, digging trenches, and dodging bullets a "daily routine," then yes, we had one!

But when we weren't fighting, we kept busy cleaning weapons, cooking, and sharing stories. Some nights, we'd sit around a small fire, singing old Indian folk songs—trying to remind ourselves of home.

Ibrahim: *What kind of food did you eat?*

Great-Grandpa: Oh, *the food!* (laughs) We mostly got British military rations—biscuits, canned meat, dried vegetables, and tea. Sometimes, if we were lucky, we got fresh chapatis made by Indian cooks. And if we were *really* lucky, we'd trade food with friendly Italian villagers for fresh bread and cheese.

Maryam (smiling): *At least there was some good food in all that hardship!*

Great-Grandpa (grinning): True, but no food ever tasted as good as the first home-cooked meal I had when I finally returned to India!

A Final Reflection

Ibrahim looked down at his notebook, realizing he had no more questions left. He had come prepared to test his Great-Grandfather, but instead, he had learned more than he ever expected.

Ibrahim (quietly): *Thank you, Great-Grandpa… for everything.*

Maryam (nodding): *Yes. We can't even imagine what you and your fellow soldiers went through.*

Great-Grandpa smiled, his eyes full of wisdom and warmth.

Great-Grandpa: My dear children, always remember—war is not about heroes or victories. It's about loss, sacrifice, and the hope for a better world. I tell you these stories not so you admire war, but so you appreciate *peace.*

For a moment, there was silence. Then, Ibrahim, trying to lighten the mood, stood up dramatically.

Ibrahim (saluting): *Commander Ibrahim declares—Great-Grandpa gets 100% marks! You are officially a war historian!*

Everyone laughed. The stories were heavy, but they had brought the family closer. Maryam and Ibrahim had learned not just about history, but about courage, sacrifice, and the true cost of war.

And as they sat together, listening to the crickets outside, they knew this was a conversation they would remember for the rest of their lives.

The Grandkids' Wartime Inquiry: A Walk Through History

Maryam and **Ibrahim** sat quietly, reflecting on the heavy yet fascinating stories their **Great-Grandpa** had shared. The room was filled with the weight of history—of battles fought, friendships lost, and a life shaped by war. Just when it seemed like the conversation was coming to an end, a small but determined voice broke the silence.

It was Yousuf, the youngest of the three, stepping forward with an eager expression.

Yousuf (tilting his head): **Great-Grandpa**... *can I ask you something too?*

Great-Grandpa, who had been sipping his coffee, chuckled.

Great-Grandpa: Oh ho! So even the little soldier wants to interrogate me? Alright, **Yousuf**, I'm ready—ask away!

Yousuf smiled mischievously. He had been listening carefully, and now it was his turn to uncover more secrets of the past.

Staying Connected with Home

Yousuf: *How did you talk to your family when you were so far away in Italy?*

Great-Grandpa (sighing): Ah, that was the hardest part, my boy. There were no phones, no internet—just letters. We would write letters on thin military paper, and it would take months to reach home. Sometimes, I wouldn't hear from my family for half a year. Can you imagine waiting that long just to know if your loved ones were safe? I personally received a handful of letters after my return home from Italy, each carrying a wave of memories and emotions.

Maryam (shaking her head): *That's so different from today. We get worried if a text takes five minutes to send!*

Great-Grandpa (smiling): Yes, times have changed. But back then, every letter was like a treasure. The moment you got one, you held onto it, reading it again and again, as if the words carried the warmth of home.

Friendships in a Foreign Land

Yousuf: *Did you make any friends in Italy?*

Great-Grandpa: Oh, absolutely! The Italian people were suffering too. Many of them hated the war and just wanted peace. Some families helped us, sharing food and shelter when they could. There was an old Italian woman who would bake fresh bread and sneak it to us soldiers—she reminded me of my own mother.

And then there were the children! Just like you three, they would run around, full of energy, curious about us. We would give them biscuits and chocolates from our rations, and in return, they would teach us Italian words.

Ibrahim (laughing): *So you can speak Italian?*

Great-Grandpa (chuckling): Just a few words! "Grazie" (thank you), "pane" (bread), and of course, "Pace" (peace). That was the most important one.

Yousuf: *How did you order Pizza in Italian?*

Great Grandpa: "Una Pizza followed by the name of Pizza.

Courage Under Fire

Yousuf: *Weren't you scared during the war? How did you manage?*

Great-Grandpa leaned forward, his expression growing thoughtful.

Great-Grandpa: Fear is always there, Yousuf. But you learn to live with it. The key is to never let fear control you. You focus on the mission, on protecting your fellow soldiers, and on surviving one more day.

But I won't lie—some nights, lying in the trenches, I would think of home. Of my mother's prayers, my father's wisdom, the streets of my village. Those thoughts gave me strength. We also prayed together, finding comfort in faith, believing that if we survived, we would return home stronger.

Maryam (softly): *You must have lost many friends, didn't you?*

Great-Grandpa (his voice heavy): Yes, too many. And that is why I always tell you… *war is never something to wish for.*

The room was silent for a moment before Yousuf continued.

The End of the War & Aftermath

Yousuf: *What was it like when the war finally ended in 1945?*

Great-Grandpa (smiling slightly): Ah, that day! May 8, 1945—Victory in Europe Day! The war was finally over. But do you know something strange?

Yousuf (curious): What?

Great-Grandpa: There was no cheering among us soldiers. No celebrations. We were happy, of course, but also exhausted. We had seen so much loss, so much destruction. The war had ended, but the scars remained.

Ibrahim: *Did you get any medals for your service?*

Great-Grandpa: Yes, I received the Italy Star and the British War Medal. But let me tell you something—medals are just metal. The real honor was in coming back alive, in being able to tell my story to you today.

Yousuf: *And what was the biggest lesson you learned from the war?*

Great-Grandpa (looking at each of them): That peace is fragile, and it must be protected at all costs. I saw what happens when people let greed and hatred take over. Wars are not fought by kings and politicians—they are fought by young men like me, who just wanted to go home.

Life After the War & Reflection

Yousuf: *How did the war change your life when you returned to India?*

Great-Grandpa (smiling): At first, it was strange. The world had changed, and so had I. I no longer cared for little things like arguments or pride—I just wanted peace and family.

I spent time rebuilding my life, learning new skills, and making sure that I never forgot the lessons of war. And most importantly, I promised myself that I would teach my children and grandchildren to value peace above all else.

Maryam (nodding): *That's why you tell us these stories, isn't it?*

Great-Grandpa (smiling warmly): Exactly, my dear. I don't tell them to glorify war—I tell them so you never wish for it.

Final Question – Did the War Change the World for Better or Worse?

Yousuf hesitated before asking his last question.

Yousuf: Looking back... *do you think the war made the world better or worse?*

Great-Grandpa sighed deeply.

Great-Grandpa: Wars are always meant to bring peace, but they only bring more wars. The world changed, yes—new nations were born, old empires fell, and technology advanced. But the cost was millions of lives.

The war was supposed to teach the world a lesson… yet even today, wars still happen. Greed and power still rule. That is why I hope that your generation will be wiser than mine. That you will learn from the past, and work towards a world where war is no longer needed.

The grandchildren sat in silence, absorbing the weight of his words.

Ibrahim (saluting again): Well, Great-Grandpa, you didn't just pass our test—you taught us something greater than any history book ever could.

Maryam (smiling): Yes. We'll never forget these stories.

Yousuf (grinning): And I'll tell my children too, so they know how brave our **Great-Grandpa** was!

Great-Grandpa chuckled, pulling them all into a warm embrace.

Great-Grandpa: That, my dear **Yousuf**, is the greatest medal I could ever receive.

The Final Question – A War for Peace?

The room fell into a deep silence. The soft glow of LED lights cast subtle shadows on the walls, as if the past itself was listening. The children, now deeply moved, sat shoulder to shoulder. This was no longer just a conversation—it had transformed into a mission, a calling from history to the future.

Maryam, Ibrahim, and Yousuf looked at each other, then turned to their **Great-Grandpa**, their voices joining in unison.

"Great-Grandpa, *some people say 'war is the only solution for peace.' Is that because they don't truly understand the destruction and horror of war? Do they not see the suffering, the loss, the shattered families? After hearing your story, we are scared—not of enemies, but of the idea that humans could still choose war. We promise you that we will never support war, whether between nations, among ethnic groups, or for the foolish ambitions of leaders who find joy in destruction."*

Great-Grandpa sat still, his eyes reflecting years of memories—some painful, some hopeful. He set down his coffee, clasped his hands together, and looked at each of them, as if engraving their young, hopeful faces in his heart. Then, he spoke, his voice filled with wisdom, sorrow, and most of all, love.

Great-Grandpa:
"My dear children, today, you have given me the greatest joy I have ever known. I have seen war, I have walked through its fire, and I have carried its wounds—not just on my body, but in my soul. And yet, you have shown me something far more powerful than war… *hope.*

Yes, some people say war brings peace. But they are wrong. War only brings silence—of the fallen, of the grieving, of the innocent lives torn apart. True peace does not come from war—it comes from understanding, from justice, from kindness.

You have spoken the words that the world desperately needs to hear. You do not wish to fight wars of bloodshed—you wish to fight wars of humanity, wars against hunger, disease, and ignorance. And that, my dear children, is the only war worth fighting.

If we must raise our voices, let it be for the poor.
If we must build armies, let them be engineers,doctors, teachers, and healers.

If we must drop anything from the sky, let it be food and medicine, not bombs.
If we must conquer anything, let it be the hatred in our own hearts.

You dream of a world where no child sleeps hungry, where clean water flows in every village, where disease is defeated, and education reaches the farthest corners of the earth. That is a dream worth fighting for. And my children, *you must never stop fighting for it.*

You see, the Creator did not place us on this beautiful Earth to destroy it. He gave us this beautiful planet, full of mountains and rivers, stars and skies, and hearts that can love. He gave us minds to build, not to burn. He gave us hands to lift others up, not to strike them down. And He gave us a voice—to speak for those who cannot speak for themselves.

If you truly want to honor my story, my struggles, my survival—then promise me this: Be the generation that ends war, not the one that repeats it.

Be the voices of peace, the builders of bridges, the healers of wounds. Work for knowledge, for justice, for kindness. Let your hands plant trees, not graves. Let your minds create cures, not weapons. And above all, never, ever forget what I have told you today. Because the greatest enemy of peace is forgetfulness."

The room was silent, but not empty. It was full—full of something invisible yet undeniable. Something powerful. Something eternal.

It was full of purpose.

Maryam wiped away a tear. **Ibrahim** nodded solemnly, his heart pounding with newfound responsibility. **Yousuf,** the youngest, clenched his fists—not in anger, but in determination.

Maryam (softly): "We promise, **Great-Grandpa**. We will be that generation."

Ibrahim: "We will fight—not with swords, but with ideas, with kindness, with unity."

Yousuf (whispering): "We will not forget." your teachings.

Great-Grandpa's lips trembled as he smiled. His eyes, which had seen so much darkness, now saw light—light in the faces of his great-grandchildren.

And in that moment, he knew…

His war was over.

But theirs—the war for a better world—had just begun.

<u>**All three children, their voices trembling with urgency, pleaded in unison**</u>

"Great Grandpa, "A Message of Peace to the Leaders of the World"

To those who forge weapons of war instead of bridges of hope—hear the voices of billions who long for peace. Yet, you remain deaf, consumed by your hunger for power. You expand your borders not with diplomacy, but with destruction, crushing the poor and seizing lands as if human lives were mere pawns in your ruthless game.

You twist justice, bending it to serve the wicked, blinded by ethnic biases and ideological fanaticism. You corrupt the very institution meant to uphold global harmony—the UN Security Council—wielding veto powers like weapons against peace itself. And then there are the nations that choose silence over courage, abstaining from crucial votes, not out of wisdom, but to sow confusion. Do they stand with justice, or are they quietly enabling tyrants who dream of ruling the world? Their silence is not neutrality—it is complicity.

History will remember not just the actions of the oppressors, but the cowardice of those who watched in silence. Will you be remembered as a builder of peace or as a bystander to destruction? The choice is yours.

Why don't they learn from history?

Did the First World War not teach them, when 15 to 22 million lives were lost and 23 million more were wounded? Did the Second World War not shake their souls, with 70 to 85 million people—civilians and soldiers alike—perishing in the flames of destruction? Did they not grieve for the 150,000 to over a million lost in Iraq? Or the 176,000 souls taken in Afghanistan? Have they forgotten Vietnam, where 2 million civilians and 1.1 million fighters perished? Did the ongoing Russia-Ukraine war not open their eyes, where nearly a million civilians and soldiers have already been killed? And now, in Gaza, where at least 46,006 Palestinians have been slaughtered, 109,373 wounded—since October 7, 2023—and still, the massacre continues!

How much more blood must be spilled before they understand?

We must send a powerful message to the world's strongest leaders—whose hands drip with the blood of innocent men, women, and children. Their thirst for war is a stain on humanity.

With tears streaming down their faces, the children sobbed uncontrollably.

"**Great Grandpa**, *we are scared—scared of what the future holds. We fear that innocent people may never truly be safe. Please, pray to the Creator. Beg Him to grant wisdom to those leaders who still walk this earth, bearing the shadow of Adolf Hitler in their hearts. Pray that their eyes open before it is too late.*

Pray for the people who elect them, who follow them blindly, unaware of the darkness they enable. May they awaken before the world is soaked in more blood. May no soul ever again be sacrificed in the name of ethnic cleansing, in the name of faith—by the very hands that were meant to shield and protect."

*"**Great Grandpa**, pray to Him—beg Him—to stop bringing beasts into this world. We don't want our beloved Earth to turn into a burning hell, a place of endless suffering. Let harmony and love prevail instead.*

Pray that the strong and the weak alike may sleep peacefully at night, without the terror of bombs tearing through their dreams. Shame upon these beasts who walk among us, who were born on this Earth only to drench it in the blood of millions—all for the sake of greed, for mere scraps of land that will one day turn to dust."

***"Great Grandpa,** why do these heartless leaders—who juggle fireballs in the name of patriotism and nationalism—not realize that one day, they too will perish, just like Hitler? Do they truly believe they are immortal, that their power will shield them from the same fate that swallowed tyrants before them?*

Why do they not see that the blood they spill today will stain the hands of history forever? That the land they fight for will not carry their names, but only the echoes of the innocent lives they destroyed? Do they not fear the day when their own graves will be forgotten, unmarked, cursed by the very people they once ruled?

*Pray for them, **Great Grandpa.** Pray that their hearts awaken before it is too late. Before they turn our world into a graveyard of dreams, where children no longer laugh and mothers cry for sons who never return. Pray that they realize—before their final breath—that no empire of hatred has ever stood the test of time, and no throne built on blood has ever escaped the judgment of the Divine."*

Their cries shook the room, piercing the very soul of **Great Grandpa**. He could hold back no longer. He gathered them into his arms, their little bodies trembling against his chest. Tears welled up in his old, weary eyes and spilled down his cheeks.

The coffee cup slipped from his trembling hands, crashing onto the floor. A dark stain spread across the carpet, but no one noticed.

A heavy silence settled over the room.

A silence that carried the weight of the world's sorrow.

A silence that begged for change.

The family room was thick with tension, the air heavy with unspoken thoughts. It was midday, yet an eerie stillness had settled over everyone. Faces were serious, brows furrowed, and no one dared to break the silence that wrapped around them like an invisible shroud. Even the usual warmth of the room felt distant, as if the very walls had absorbed the weight of the conversation.

Sensing the unease, **Great Grandpa** leaned back in his chair, exhaling slowly. He knew that pressing on wouldn't help for the time being. Some conversations were best left to settle before being revisited with a clearer mind. With a wise nod, he made a decision. "Let's stop here for now," he said, his voice calm yet firm. "We'll continue our discussion after the lunch break, but with lighter minds and a different tone. A full stomach often brings a fresh perspective."

The children, who had been unusually quiet, exchanged glances before slipping away upstairs, their minds already shifting gears. Their excitement returned as they prepared for a much-awaited weekend lunch, a family tradition they always looked forward to. Meanwhile, **Great Grandpa** remained seated for a moment, gazing out the window. Some conversations were heavy, but life had a way of balancing things—serious moments today, joyous ones tomorrow. And that was the beauty of it all.

Upstairs, the children freshened up, their earlier tension slowly dissolving. Downstairs, the air filled with the mouthwatering aroma of spices and slow-cooked delights. In the kitchen, Grandma and Mother worked in harmony, preparing a grand feast. The rich fragrance of Chicken Biryani mingled with the sweetness of a special dessert—chocolate cake paired with creamy ice cream, a combination the children adored on weekends.

Great Grandpa's stomach rumbled in anticipation, making him chuckle to himself. If there was one thing that could lift the spirits of a family, it was a well-cooked meal shared with love. Soon, the dining table was set, dishes placed with care, and the call to gather echoed through the house.

The weekend lunch was nothing short of a feast. Laughter and cheerful chatter replaced the earlier silence as everyone savored the delicious meal. The children, their spirits now high, eagerly took second helpings, while Great Grandpa enjoyed each bite with deep appreciation. As the last crumbs disappeared and plates were cleared, the children and Great Grandpa turned to Grandma and Mother with grateful smiles.

"That was amazing!" one of the children beamed.

"Yes! Thank you for this wonderful meal," **Great Grandpa** added warmly.

Grandma and Mother exchanged smiles, their hearts full. Nothing was more rewarding than seeing the family happy and together.

With satisfied stomachs and lighter hearts, the family was ready to embrace the rest of the day, knowing that even the heaviest of discussions could be balanced with love, warmth, and, of course, a good meal.

After a little while, Grandma arrived with a steaming cup of black coffee, its rich aroma filling the air. This time, she had carefully chosen a shining blue mug—**Great Grandpa**'s favorite, a subtle gesture he always appreciated. With a satisfied smile, he wrapped his hands around the warm cup, savoring the moment he had been waiting for.

Just then, the sound of hurried footsteps echoed through the house as the children descended the stairs, their energy restored and curiosity reignited. As they entered the family room, a renewed sense of anticipation filled the space. The stage was set once again, ready for the afternoon conversation to resume.

Yousuf, brimming with excitement, took the lead for the second session of their conversation with **Great-Grandpa.** The great-grandchildren had gathered around him, eager to unravel the mystery of his remarkable health and energy.

The Secret of Great-Grandpa's Good Health

Yousuf cleared his throat and spoke with admiration,
"Great-Grandpa, *we are all amazed at how fit and energetic you are even at this stage of life—touch wood! We want to uncover the secrets behind your health so that we can follow in your footsteps and live a long, happy life like you. Would you kindly share your wisdom with us?"*

Great-Grandpa chuckled, his eyes twinkling.
"Ah, so you all want to steal my secrets, huh? Well, I won't make it too easy for you!" he said playfully.
The children giggled, eager for his answers.

Yousuf: "Great-Grandpa, *what kind of food did you eat when you were a child?"*

Great-Grandpa smiled nostalgically.
Oh, back in my time, we didn't have fancy junk food like you kids do today! We ate fresh, home-cooked meals made with love. Our diet was simple but nutritious—lots of lentils, vegetables, homemade yogurt, fresh fruits, and whole grains. And let me tell you, nothing tasted better than the mangoes we plucked straight from the trees!

Yousuf (excitedly): *Were there any special home remedies your parents or grandparents used to keep you healthy?*

Great-Grandpa nodded.
"Absolutely! Whenever we caught a cold, my grandmother would make us drink warm turmeric milk, and it worked like magic. For digestion, we had fennel seeds. And if we ever had a minor wound, honey and turmeric were our go-to medicines. We relied on nature a lot more than medicines in those days."

Yousuf (curious): *What games or activities did you play as a child that kept you active?*

Great-Grandpa laughed heartily.
"Oh, we were always running around! We played kabaddi, hide-and-seek, gilli-danda, and climbed trees like little monkeys. We didn't have video games or mobile phones, so we spent all our time outdoors, running, jumping, and cycling. That's why we were never lazy or tired!"

Yousuf: *And what about now,* **Great-Grandpa**? *Do you follow a fixed routine for eating, sleeping, and exercising?*

Great-Grandpa nodded.
"Yes, my dear. Discipline is key. I wake up early, offer my prayers, take a morning walk, and eat a balanced diet. I never overeat, and I always go to bed on time. Your body is like a machine—take care of it properly, and it will serve you well for a long time!"

Yousuf (wide-eyed): *How do you stay so energetic even now?*

Great-Grandpa smiled.
"The secret is simple—keep moving, keep laughing, and stay stress-free. I don't let worries take over my mind. I enjoy every moment, whether it's talking to you all, playing a game, or reading a book. Energy comes from a happy heart!"

Yousuf: *Do you believe waking up early in the morning has helped you stay fit?*

Great-Grandpa raised an eyebrow.
"Oh, absolutely! The early morning air is fresh, peaceful, and full of blessings. Waking up early gives me time to exercise, plan my day, and start with a calm mind. Try it—you'll feel the difference!"

Yousuf (grinning): *Have you ever followed any strict fitness regimen, or is it just natural for you?*

Great-Grandpa chuckled.
"No fancy gyms for me! My fitness comes from a simple lifestyle—walking, stretching, eating right, and staying active throughout the day. The secret is consistency, not intensity. A little effort every day goes a long way."

Yousuf: *What do you do to keep your mind sharp and active?*

Great-Grandpa tapped his temple playfully.
"Ah, the mind is like a muscle—it needs exercise too! I read books, solve puzzles, play chess, and, most importantly, I keep learning new things. And do you know what else keeps my mind sharp?"
The children leaned in, eager for the answer.

"Talking to you all! Keeping up with young, curious minds keeps my brain young too!" he said with a wink.

The great-grandchildren burst into laughter, feeling both inspired and entertained. They realized that their Great-Grandpa's secret to good health was not just about food and exercise—it was about staying happy, active, and connected with loved ones.

"Thank you, **Great-Grandpa!** We promise to follow your advice and take care of our health just like you!" **Yousuf** said sincerely.

Great-Grandpa patted his head affectionately.
That's the spirit, my dear ones. A healthy life is a happy life, and I want you all to live long, strong, and full of joy!

The Mystery of Great-Grandpa's Health – Ibrahim's Turn!

- After **Yousuf's** turn, the ever-curious **Ibrahim** couldn't hold back any longer. He jumped in front, straightened his imaginary tie, and dramatically announced,
- "Okay, everyone, now it's **my** turn! **Great-Grandpa,** I'm about to unleash a rapid-fire round of questions. You have to answer honestly—no secrets!"
- **Great-Grandpa** chuckled, folding his arms. "Oh, so now I'm on trial? Let's see if I can survive this interrogation!"
- **Ibrahim** laughed, eager to dig into the secrets of **Great-Grandpa's health.**

Diet & Nutrition

- **Ibrahim: Great-Grandpa**, what kind of food do you eat every day to stay healthy?
- **Great-Grandpa grinned.** Ah, my secret potion! Simple home-cooked meals. Lentils, vegetables, whole grains, and fruits. I eat like a king at breakfast, like a prince at lunch, and like a beggar at dinner. That's the trick!
- **Ibrahim** (confused): *Why eat like a beggar at dinner?*
- **Great-Grandpa** winked. "Because if you stuff yourself at night, your stomach will protest louder than a car alarm! Light dinner, deep sleep. Heavy dinner, nightmare feast!"
- **Ibrahim:** *Do you avoid any particular food that you think is harmful?*
- **Great-Grandpa** nodded. Oh yes! Anything too oily, too sugary, or too processed. Basically, anything that looks too tempting is probably trouble.
- **Ibrahim** (grinning): *So, no pizzas, no burgers?*
- **Great-Grandpa** sighed dramatically. Oh, I've had my fair share of them, but they don't love me back! My stomach and I signed a peace treaty: I treat it well, and it doesn't rebel!

- **Ibrahim:** *Do you eat sweets or fast food, or have you always stayed away from them?*
- **Great-Grandpa** smiled mischievously. Oh, I do love sweets! But I follow the 'One Bite Happiness Rule'—one bite is happiness, two bites are enjoyment, three bites… Well, then my belly starts planning revenge.
- **Ibrahim:** *What are your favorite fruits, vegetables, and drinks that help in maintaining good health?*
- **Great-Grandpa beamed.** Fruits? Mangoes, bananas, and pomegranates—they're nature's candy! Vegetables? Spinach and carrots—they make you strong and sharp. And drinks? Water! Lots and lots of water. Remember, if you drink enough water, your body thanks you. If you don't, it gets cranky like a baby!
- **Ibrahim:** *Do you believe in herbal or natural medicines? Have you ever used them?*
- **Great-Grandpa nodded.** "Oh, absolutely! Herbal remedies are like old friends—they may smell weird, but they never let you down. Honey, turmeric, ginger… these are my superheroes. No capes, but full of powers!"

Health & Wellness

- **Ibrahim:** Have you ever been seriously ill? If yes, how did you recover so well?
- **Great-Grandpa** sighed dramatically. Oh, I've had my battles! Fevers, coughs, even a few surprises from my stomach that I'd rather not talk about! But the trick is—don't panic, eat well, rest, and let the body do its magic.
- **Ibrahim:** *So, no rushing to the doctor for every little thing?*
- **Great-Grandpa** shook his head. Nope! If it's serious, sure, but for small things, let the body fight its own battles. The immune system is like a lazy soldier—if you don't train it, it forgets how to fight!
- **Ibrahim:** *How do you manage stress or worries?*

- **Great-Grandpa** smiled. Oh, stress? I have a simple formula: If you can fix it, fix it. If you can't fix it, forget it. And if it's beyond your control, why worry? It's like trying to stop the rain with an umbrella full of holes!
- **Ibrahim:** *But what if something really worries you?*
- **Great-Grandpa** shrugged. Then I do my favorite stress-buster: I talk to you, play chess, or eat a mango or banana. Works every time.
- **Ibrahim:** *Do you follow any special breathing exercises, yoga, or meditation?*
- **Great-Grandpa nodded.** Oh yes! Deep breathing is my favorite. I call it the 'Grandpa Recharge'—breathe in, hold, breathe out, and poof! Stress gone.
- **Ibrahim:** *Does it really work?*
- **Great-Grandpa** winked. Try it. If it doesn't work, you can always blame me and eat an extra piece of cake to feel better.
- **Ibrahim:** *What is your secret to a good night's sleep?*
- **Great-Grandpa s**tretched and yawned playfully. Simple! No late-night snacks, no overthinking, and no staring at those glowing screens before bed. I let my mind rest like a baby wrapped in a cozy blanket.
- **Ibrahim** (giggling): *What if you can't sleep?*
- **Great-Grandpa** grinned. Then I count sheep. If that doesn't work, I imagine you kids causing trouble… and suddenly, I'm exhausted!
- **Ibrahim** burst into laughter.
- **Ibrahim:** *How do you keep a positive attitude toward life?*
- **Great-Grandpa** leaned in closer, his voice warm. Life is a big, colorful story, my dear **Ibrahim.** Some pages are happy, some are sad, and some are just plain funny. The key is to laugh more, love more, and always believe that tomorrow is another chance to make great memories.
- **Ibrahim** clapped, inspired and entertained.

- Thank you, **Great-Grandpa!** I'm going to follow your advice... and maybe even steal your 'One Bite Happiness Rule' for sweets!
- **Great-Grandpa** laughed heartily. Go ahead, my little rascal! Just remember—good health is a gift, so take care of it and enjoy every moment.

With that, Ibrahim's session came to a close, but his wisdom and laughter echoed in their hearts, leaving behind cherished memories to treasure forever.

The Grand Finale – Maryam's Turn

After **Yousuf** and **Ibrahim** had their fun, it was time for **Maryam**, the sharpest of them all, to take the stage. Unlike the boys, who fired their questions like playful detectives, Maryam approached with the elegance of a scholar about to present a thesis.

She stepped forward, adjusting her imaginary glasses, cleared her throat like a professor about to give a lecture, and said,

"**Great-Grandpa,** *may I have your permission to begin?*

Great-Grandpa, amused by her formality, chuckled and nodded. "Permission granted, **Professor Maryam.** Let the questioning begin!

Maryam smiled, took a deep breath, and started her session like a true genius student in a classroom.

Secrets to Longevity

- **Maryam:** *What advice would you give us to stay as healthy and strong as you are*?
- **Great-Grandpa** leaned back, stroking his chin. Ah, the million-dollar question! The answer is simple—eat well, move often,

sleep soundly, and most importantly, don't take life too seriously! Stress is like a mosquito—it's small but annoyingly dangerous. Keep it away, and you'll live longer.

- **Maryam** (smiling): *So, no stress at all?*
- **Great-Grandpa** laughed. Well, a little stress is good—it keeps you on your toes! But worrying about things you can't change? That's like arguing with a stubborn parrot—it gets you nowhere!
- **Maryam:** *Do you think modern lifestyles are unhealthy compared to the way you lived?*
- **Great-Grandpa** sighed. Oh, absolutely! Back in my day, we walked more, played outside, and ate real food—not things that come in plastic wrappers with names we can't pronounce! These days, people exercise their thumbs on their phones more than their legs!
- **Maryam** (grinning): *So, should we throw away our phones?*
- **Great-Grandpa** smirked. No, no, keep them! Just don't let them keep you! Use them wisely—don't let them steal your sleep, your time, or your real-life connections.
- **Maryam:** *What are the three most important habits that everyone should adopt for a long and healthy life?*
- **Great-Grandpa** raised three fingers. One—Eat natural foods and drink plenty of water. Two—Move your body every single day, even if it's just a walk. Three—Laugh, my dear! Laughter is the cheapest and best medicine. No side effects, except maybe a sore stomach from laughing too much!
- **Maryam:** *Do you really believe happiness and laughter contribute to good health?*
- **Great-Grandpa** clapped his hands. Oh, without a doubt! A joyful heart keeps you young. If you frown too much, life frowns back. But if you laugh, life laughs with you!
- **Maryam** (giggling): *So, if I laugh all day, will I never get sick?*
- **Great-Grandpa** chuckled. Well, you still need good food and sleep! But if you mix laughter with healthy habits, you'll be unstoppable—just like me!

Reflection on Life

Maryam: *Looking back, what choices do you think helped you maintain good health over the years?*

Great-Grandpa took a deep breath, as if traveling back in time. Discipline, my dear. I never abused my body with bad habits. No smoking, no overeating, no laziness. I respected my body, and in return, my body respected me. It's a two-way deal.

Maryam (thoughtful): *If you could give your younger self one piece of advice about health and lifestyle, what would it be?*

Great-Grandpa smiled. Take care of your body early! Young people think they're invincible, eating junk, skipping sleep, and sitting all day. But guess what? Your body keeps a record of everything. One day, it sends you the bill. And trust me, that bill isn't cheap!

Maryam: *That's a bit scary!*

Great-Grandpa laughed. It should be! But don't worry—if you take care of yourself now, you won't have to pay a heavy price later.

Maryam: *What are the most important values or lessons about life and health that you want us to follow?*

Great-Grandpa's eyes twinkled as he leaned forward. Ah, now we're talking about the real treasures of life!

He raised one finger. "First—Respect your body. It's the only one you'll ever have."

Then a second. "Second—Respect your mind. Feed it with good thoughts, not negativity."

And finally, a third. "Third—Respect your time. Use it wisely, don't waste it on useless worries or distractions."

Maryam nodded, taking mental notes.

As **she** finished, she looked up at **Great-Grandpa** with admiration.

Thank you, **Great-Grandpa. T**his has been the best class ever!

Great-Grandpa chuckled. Oh, I didn't know I was teaching a class! But if you learned something, that makes me the happiest teacher in the world.

The rest of the grandchildren clapped, and **Yousuf** and **Ibrahim j**okingly saluted their wise **Great-Grandpa.**

Alright, class dismissed! Now, who's up for a game of Ludo? **Great-Grandpa** declared, laughing.

The children cheered, and just like that, the lesson turned into another moment of fun, filled with joy, laughter, and love—exactly as **Great-Grandpa** had always advised.

The Final Challenge – A Test for Great-Grandpa's Wisdom

After an engaging and laughter-filled conversation**, the great-grandchildren** still weren't fully satisfied. They looked at each other, nodding in agreement—there was one final challenge for their beloved **Great-Grandpa.**

"Great-Grandpa," Yousuf spoke up first, "your advice is valuable, but it mostly fits the time when you were young. The world has changed. Life is much faster, and people don't have time to follow those old habits."

Ibrahim added, *We live in a world where technology controls everything. People are glued to their phones, work late hours, eat fast food, and* *don't have time for proper sleep or exercise. Pollution is everywhere, natural food is disappearing, and stress is increasing. How do we balance all this?*

Maryam, always the sharp one, leaned forward. **Great-Grandpa**, *we want real solutions—something practical that fits today's lifestyle. How can we stay healthy and happy in this modern, chaotic world?*

The great-grandchildren looked at him expectantly, their eyes filled with curiosity and a bit of skepticism. Could **Great-Grandpa's** *wisdom still stand the test of time?*

Great-Grandpa's Timeless Wisdom

Great-Grandpa smiled and adjusted his glasses. He could see the genuine concern in their eyes. The world has indeed changed, but the fundamentals of a good life never do. He cleared his throat and began:

"My dear ones, you are right—the world is different now. But tell me, has the human body changed? Does it no longer need proper food, sleep, and movement? Does the mind no longer need peace? No matter how advanced we become, our bodies and minds still function the same way as they did centuries ago. The only difference is that now, we are ignoring their needs in the name of progress."

The children fell silent, absorbing his words.

"Let me give you some modern-day solutions that fit your lifestyle," he continued.

Balancing Modern Life with Healthy Habits

1. Limited Time? Make Smart Choices!

"If you don't have time for long workouts, at least move often."

- Take the stairs instead of the elevator.
- Walk while talking on the phone.
- Stretch every hour if you sit too long.
- Do quick exercises at home—just 10 minutes a day is better than nothing!

2. No Time to Cook? Choose Wisely!

"Fast food may be easy, but health is priceless."

- If you must eat out, choose grilled over fried, water over soda, and fresh over processed.
- Carry nuts, fruits, or yogurt instead of chips and cookies.
- Learn simple one-pot recipes that take less time but are healthier than packaged food.

3. Too Much Screen Time? Control It Before It Controls You!

"Technology is your servant, not your master."

- Set screen-free hours, especially before bedtime.
- Use apps that limit social media time instead of scrolling endlessly.
- Take breaks—every 30 minutes, look away from the screen and stretch.

4. Sleep is Non-Negotiable!

"You can survive a day without Netflix or Cartoon Network but not without sleep!"

- Fix your sleep schedule—even 6-7 hours of deep sleep is better than 10 hours of disturbed sleep.
- Power down your screens at least 30 minutes before bedtime and step into a world of relaxation. Dive into a good book, let calming music wash over you, or lose yourself in the warmth of

Grandma's soothing bedtime stories—her voice weaving magic as you drift into peaceful dreams.

- Keep your bedroom dark, quiet, and cool for better sleep quality.

5. Pollution & Stress? Protect Yourself!

"If the air outside is bad, make the air inside better."

- Keep plants at home—they clean the air.
- Drink lots of water to flush out toxins.
- Practice deep breathing—it relaxes the mind and strengthens the lungs.

6. Career & Stress? Learn to Manage It!

"Your job is important, but your health is more important."

- Prioritize tasks; don't do everything at once.
- Take small breaks; breathe, stretch, relax.
- Don't bring work stress home—find time to laugh with family.

7. Money is Tight? Health is Still Possible!

"Good health doesn't need to be expensive."

- Walking is free.
- Cooking at home is cheaper than eating out.
- Smiling costs nothing, but stress can cost your health.

8. Too Many Diseases? Strengthen Your Immunity!

"You can't control all diseases, but you can control your body's defense system."

- Eat more natural foods—fruits, vegetables, and homemade meals, avoid processed food.

- Choose fresh, organic vegetables and fruits to nourish your body with nature's best. And if you have a little space, why not create your own backyard garden? With a little love and help from Mummy and Papa, you can grow your own delicious, homegrown goodness—fresh from the earth to your plate!
- Drink herbal teas instead of sugary drinks.
- Keep your mind happy—stress weakens immunity.

Final Words from Great-Grandpa

Great-Grandpa looked at each of them with warmth. **"Children,** you don't have to live exactly like I did. But if you ignore your health today, you will pay the price tomorrow. Balance is the key. Work hard, but take Take care of your body—it's the only place you have to live. Embrace technology, but don't let it rule your life. Nourish yourself with wholesome food, stay active every day, and most importantly, fill your heart with laughter and joy. And always be grateful to the Creator of the universe, who has blessed you with the beauty of nature and an abundance of gifts to live a life of peace, happiness, and good health.

The great-grandchildren nodded, realizing that his wisdom wasn't old-fashioned—it was timeless.

"Alright, **Great-Grandpa," Maryam** said with a smile. "You win! Your advice does fit in our modern world!"

Great-Grandpa chuckled. "Of course, it does! Now, who's up for a game of chess? Or should I just start telling a funny story?"

The room burst into laughter, and just like that, wisdom and fun blended together—a perfect balance, just as **Great-Grandpa** had taught them.

The Conversation Reaches Its Final Note

By this time, everyone looked exhausted. Their minds were full of deep thoughts, and their heads were spinning with **Great-Grandpa's** wisdom. Even the most energetic among them, **Ibrahim**, leaned back and stretched his arms.

Maryam sighed dramatically, "**Great-Grandpa**, my brain is overloaded! I need time to process all this wisdom before my circuits crash!"

Yousuf rubbed his eyes, Phew! *Who knew learning about life could be this exhausting?*

Even **Great-Grandpa** chuckled, noticing their drained expressions. He leaned forward, placing his hands on his knees, and said, "Well, well, my young philosophers! It seems like your minds have eaten more food for thought than your stomachs ever could!"

Everyone laughed, but their tired faces couldn't hide the truth—they needed a break.

Great-Grandpa stretched his arms, yawned, and nodded. "Alright, children, I agree. Too much wisdom in one day can give even the strongest minds a headache. Let's adjourn this meeting of the 'Wise and the Curious' until next Saturday."

Ibrahim raised an eyebrow, "Same time, same place?"

Great-Grandpa winked, "Of course! But come prepared—because next time, I might just test you on today's lessons!"

A wave of groans filled the room. "Oh no, a **Great-Grandpa** exam?!" **Maryam** clutched her head, pretending to faint.

Yousuf grinned, Well, at least your questions are more interesting than school tests!

As they got up to leave, **Great-Grandpa** gave a parting smile and said, "Remember, children, wisdom is like a treasure—you must carry it carefully and use it wisely. Now go, rest your brains, and come back next Saturday with more questions... and a bigger appetite for knowledge!"

With that, the session wrapped up on a joyful note, leaving everyone smiling and already looking forward to the next heartwarming conversation with their wise and witty **Great-Grandpa.** As the children hugged him tightly one last time, their hearts brimmed with love and admiration. They departed with a sense of warmth, cherishing every moment spent with him, and whispered heartfelt prayers, wishing him a long, healthy life—one that stretches another hundred years, filled with laughter, wisdom, and endless stories.

Session Two

Embark on a Cosmic Journey

Great Grandpa and the Kids Explore Astronomy with Fun and Fascinating Q&A

Astronomy

1. Stars and Constellations & Cosmic Fireworks

As usual, **Great Grandpa** wakes up at the crack of dawn, long before the sun stretches its golden arms across the sky. With a trusty wooden walking stick in one hand, clad in his well-worn but ever-reliable PT shoes and his signature coat with a cozy neck cover, he steps out for his morning walk. The garden, still wrapped in the hush of early morning, welcomes him like an old friend. He takes a few rounds, nodding at the sleepy flowers and the gossiping birds, before heading back home, feeling fresh and alive.

Back in his little haven, he carefully prepares his cherished black coffee—his morning elixir—using the microwave with the precision of a scientist in a lab. He pours it into his favorite white mug, replaces his coat with a warm, familiar gown, and settles into his beloved armchair. Ah, bliss! With each sip, the rich aroma of coffee swirls around him, blending with the quiet joy of solitude—until, of course, the weekend magic begins!

Today is special. It's the weekend, and that means one thing—his delightful, ever-curious great-grandchildren will soon come storming in like a whirlwind of joy and endless questions! He can already imagine the lively conversations ahead—stories of his time, woven with wisdom and wonder, and their eager inquiries about the marvels of modern technology and science.

And then—it happens! The spell of morning silence is broken by the sweetest sound in the world—excited chattering, hurried footsteps echoing down the staircase, filling the quiet house with life. A chorus of bright, cheerful voices rings out—"Good morning, **Great Grandpa**!"

His heart leaps with joy! He stands up, his face beaming, arms wide open, ready to embrace his little bundles of happiness. The house, which a moment ago was wrapped in calm, now brims with laughter, warmth, and the magical bond between generations. The weekend has officially begun!

Mariyam, the eldest, lingered near the armrest, her face thoughtful. "**Great Grandpa**," she began, her voice tinged with frustration, "I couldn't sleep well last night."

"Why, my dear?" he asked, concerned about creasing his brow.

"Ibrahim," she said, shooting her younger brother a teasing glare, "kept asking about shooting stars. He wouldn't stop, and I didn't know how to answer him!"

Great Grandpa threw his head back in laughter, his voice filling the room like music. "Ah, the wonders of the night sky! **Ibrahim**, you've got a curious mind, don't you?" he said, ruffling the boy's hair.

"I just want to know where they come from," **Ibrahim** said earnestly, his wide eyes glinting with curiosity.

Great Grandpa leaned back, a twinkle in his eye. "Well, my dear ones, perhaps we journey through the stars together and uncover their secrets. But first, how about we finish our morning coffee and settle in for a tale?"

The children nodded eagerly, their earlier sleepiness forgotten, as they huddled closer to **Great Grandpa**. The stage was set for another enchanting morning of shared stories, wisdom, and laughter between generations.

The excitement in the room was palpable as the children eagerly prepared for their morning session with **Great Grandpa**. But just as they settled in, he raised a hand, his wise eyes twinkling with a mix of authority and humor. “Hold on, my little explorers,” he said, leaning slightly forward. “Before we dive into stories and questions, I must remind you—no mission can start on an empty stomach!”

The children glanced at each other, realizing he was right. With a playful nod, **Great Grandpa** added, “A proper breakfast will fuel your curious minds, and I’ll need you sharp if we’re to make this a memorable session.”

The trio sprang to their feet, giggling as they hurried to the kitchen. “Mama, breakfast, please!” they chimed in unison, their voices carrying a blend of urgency and excitement. Moments later, they returned, their cheeks flushed and bellies full, ready to embark on their morning adventure.

Now seated comfortably around **Great Grandpa**’s armchair, the children were all smiles, their anticipation bubbling over. **Ibrahim**, unable to contain himself, bounced slightly in his seat. **Maryam**, ever the composed one, smoothed her dress and leaned in, her expression a mix of curiosity and readiness. **Yousuf**, nestled by **Great Grandpa**’s side, clung to his arm with wide-eyed wonder.

Great Grandpa took a deep breath, his playful smile spreading wide as a glimmer of mischief danced in his eyes. “Ah, so you’re all ready for another round of curiosity, are you?” he asked, his tone dripping with mock seriousness. He stroked his beard thoughtfully, as if pondering a great mystery himself, though his mind was already abuzz with anticipation.

“What could these bright little explorers have up their sleeves today?” he mused silently, his heart swelling with pride. But this wasn’t any ordinary storyteller sitting before them—**Great Grandpa** was well-prepared for their insatiable curiosity. Over the years, he had immersed himself in the wonders of the universe, poring over technical journals, magazines, and the latest discoveries from the worlds of astronomy, cosmology, and cutting-edge technology.

From planets to galaxies, black holes to solar systems, his knowledge spanned the cosmos, ready to be unraveled for his eager audience. He was not just their great-grandpa but their guide to the mysteries of the universe—a treasure trove of wisdom waiting to be explored. With a twinkle in his eye, he leaned forward, ready to ignite their imaginations once more.

Though excitement coursed through him, a flicker of uncertainty danced across **Great Grandpa's** face. What if their questions veered into realms he hadn't yet explored? What if their boundless curiosity unearthed gaps in his vast reservoir of knowledge? For a moment, the weight of this thought pressed upon him. But then, almost as if on cue, he let out a soft, knowing chuckle, his eyes twinkling with the wisdom of a life that had seen nearly a century of change.

"Surely," he thought, "I can meet their questions with the stories I've lived, the lessons I've learned, and the insights only time can offer."

Yet, beneath this outward confidence, a faint shadow of self-doubt lingered. How drastically the world had transformed since his youth! Back then, learning was a journey—a slow, deliberate process guided by dusty books, wise mentors, and life's trials and triumphs. There were no glowing screens or algorithms to deliver answers in milliseconds. His world had been a tapestry of patience, persistence, and discovery.

The tools his great-grandchildren wielded with such ease were, to him, the stuff of science fiction. Smartphones that held the world's knowledge, tablets brimming with interactive lessons, and social media platforms that connected continents in an instant—all these were inventions that had reshaped humanity's relationship with knowledge. Travel, once a laborious ordeal, now shrank the globe, while real-time conversations across oceans became as effortless as breathing.

And yet, amidst all this progress, he knew something they didn't—how to thrive without these marvels. In his time, imagination filled the gaps technology couldn't. Letters carried emotions, not emojis; journeys were measured in resilience, not in flight hours. Every achievement, no matter how small, was a testament to grit and ingenuity.

As he gazed at his great-grandchildren, their faces lit with the glow of curiosity and youthful wonder, a mix of pride and trepidation washed over him. Their questions would undoubtedly push him, challenge him to think, and perhaps even teach him something new. But he also knew this: while their gadgets could provide data, only he could offer wisdom—born not just of facts but of lived experience.

He reminded himself of his own story—a retired army officer who had faced situations demanding courage, adaptability, and quick thinking. He had navigated through eras of war and peace, tackled challenges without the crutch of modern tools, and emerged stronger. If he could lead men into uncertainty, he could surely guide these bright young minds with love and knowledge.

Straightening his posture, he dismissed the faint remnants of doubt. "These kids may have access to the universe at their fingertips," he thought, "but I carry the stories of a universe that can't be Googled."

And so, with a smile that spoke of quiet confidence, he prepared to bridge the vast expanse between generations. He wasn't here to compete with their modern world but to complement it, to serve as a bridge between yesterday's wisdom and tomorrow's aspirations.

As he readied himself for the cascade of questions, he murmured, "Let's see how this unfolds. They bring their tablets, laptops, and infinite curiosity, and I'll bring my stories, my lessons, and a lifetime of wonder. Together, we'll make magic."

The stage was set. The past and future were about to converge in the most delightful and enlightening way, with Great Grandpa at the helm, ready to inspire, engage, and remind his great-grandchildren that the most profound answers often come from the heart, not the screen.

"Alright, my inquisitive team," he said, his tone warm and inviting, "ask away! Together, we'll unravel the mysteries you've been holding onto."

The children beamed, their excitement now contagious, as **Great Grandpa** leaned back into his armchair. The room felt alive, brimming with the promise of stories, questions, and a morning of shared wonder.

The family room buzzed with excitement as the children's voices filled the air, their curiosity about shooting stars taking center stage. They eagerly shared how they had stayed up late, watching the mysterious streaks of light through their bedroom window.

"**Great Grandpa**, ***what are shooting stars? Are they real stars falling from the sky?" Mariyam asked, her eyes wide with wonder.***

"Why do they move so fast? Are they trying to escape something?" added Ibrahim, his tone both curious and a little nervous.

"Can they fall on our house? I was scared one might land on our bed!" Yousuf chimed in, his voice tinged with concern.

"Do stars break apart like that, or is it something else happening in the sky?" Mariyam pressed further, seeking answers.

"Is there a religious meaning behind shooting stars, or is it just a natural thing that happens?" Ibrahim asked thoughtfully.

"Do they get weaker over time and then fall, or are they pulled by stronger stars and destroyed?" Yousuf wondered, his imagination running wild.

Each question brimmed with innocence and awe, reflecting their young minds' endless thirst for knowledge. It was clear that **Great Grandpa** had a lot to explain to satisfy their curiosity.

"**Great Grandpa**, ***are shooting stars the same as meteorites? Do they hit the ground? And what about meteors—are they different from meteorites that fall to Earth?"***

Great Grandpa leaned back in his armchair, his white beard catching the soft glow of the filtered sunlight. He took a thoughtful sip of his steaming coffee, letting the children's eager voices settle. With a warm smile and a twinkle of wisdom in his eyes, he began to speak, his voice steady and calm, drawing them into his world of knowledge.

"Well, my little stars," he began with a twinkle in his eye, his voice playful yet full of wisdom. "Let's uncover this cosmic mystery together. While I may not know everything, I'll share what I've learned about the wonders of the sky and the magic of those streaking lights you spotted."

He leaned forward slightly, adding with a sense of awe, "You see, brilliant astronomers and scientists across the globe are working tirelessly, day and night, to understand these mysteries of the universe. Every streak of light, every strange occurrence in space, brings us closer to discoveries and incredible insights about our vast, ever-changing cosmos. Isn't that amazing?"

The **children** leaned in closer, their excitement palpable. They were ready to journey through the universe guided by their great-grandpa's fascinating storytelling.

Great Grandpa leaned back in his armchair, his warm smile inviting curiosity. With a sparkle in his eye, he began weaving the answers into an engaging tale.

"Ah, my dear M**ariyam**," he said, his voice gentle yet full of excitement, "shooting stars may look magical, but they're not stars at all. They're tiny pieces of space dust or rock, called meteoroids, that wander through space. When they come close to Earth, they're pulled by its gravity and rush into our atmosphere. Moving at incredible speeds, they heat up to over 2,000 degrees Celsius due to friction with the air, causing them to glow brightly and streak across the sky. That glowing trail is what we call a meteor. Isn't it amazing that something so small can create such a breathtaking display?"

He paused to let their awe settle, then added, "These meteors move so fast because they carry the speed they gained in space—sometimes tens of thousands of miles per hour! Earth's gravity pulls them even faster as they enter its atmosphere. As they vaporize, they leave behind glowing trails of gas and melted particles called trains. These trains swirl into fascinating shapes as high-altitude winds scatter them across the sky. Isn't that a beautiful dance of nature?"

Turning to **Ibrahim**, he said, "They're not trying to escape anything. It's just physics at work—their speed and Earth's pull working together to create the spectacular show we see."

Great Grandpa smiled warmly at **Yousuf**, reaching out to gently ruffle his hair. "Don't worry, little one," he said with a reassuring tone. "Most meteoroids are so tiny that they burn up completely in the atmosphere before they ever reach the ground. Only a few larger ones survive the fiery journey and become meteorites, and it's extremely rare for one to land anywhere near people—let alone in our house. You're perfectly safe."

After a thoughtful pause, he added, "Though, there are a few remarkable stories in history. Like Ann Elizabeth Fowler Hodges—on November 30, 1954, a piece of the Sylacauga meteorite crashed through her roof in Oak Grove, Alabama. It weighed about 8 pounds and left her with a nasty bruise. That was the first documented case in the U.S. of someone being injured by a meteorite. And yes, there have even been reports of meteorites landing on beds. But these events are so rare they're like winning a lottery—only, not the fun kind!"

He turned back to **Mariyam** to address her next question. "Stars, my dear, are much too massive to break apart like that. What you see are tiny fragments of space debris burning up. Stars live for millions or billions of years, shining steadily from their place in the cosmos. The shooting stars you see are far, far smaller."

To **Ibrahim**'s thoughtful query, **Great Grandpa** replied with a warm smile, "Some people like to see shooting stars as symbols of hope or divine messages, and that's a beautiful way to think about the universe. Scientifically, though, they're just cosmic dust burning up in Earth's atmosphere—a fascinating natural phenomenon. Isn't it amazing how science and imagination can blend?"

Pausing thoughtfully, he added, "In Islam, shooting stars and meteors carry a unique spiritual significance. They're described in the Quran as soldiers of Allah, protecting the heavens from eavesdroppers trying to steal divine secrets. For example, in *Surah As-Saffat* (37:10), *Surah Al-Hijr* (15:18), and *Surah Al-Jinn* (72:8-9), it's said they repel those who attempt to overhear what's above. Interestingly, this concept has parallels in earlier Jewish traditions and even Zoroastrian mythology. It's incredible how cultures across time have found ways to explain the mysteries of the sky."

Finally, he turned to **Yousuf**, his voice filled with gentle wisdom. "Meteoroids don't get weaker over time, my little explorer. They burn up because of the intense friction as they race through the atmosphere. It's not that they're destroyed by other stars or pulled apart by something stronger; it's Earth's gravity and atmosphere doing their work."

With a soft chuckle, he concluded, "And yes, meteorites are the pieces of meteoroids that survive their fiery journey and hit the ground. Meteors, on the other hand, are what you see glowing in the sky. So the next time you see a shooting star, remember—you're witnessing a tiny piece of the universe saying hello in the most spectacular way!"

The great-grandchildren, their eyes sparkling with curiosity, leaned forward, and **Mariyam** asked eagerly, "**Great Grandpa**, ***do you know if meteorites have ever fallen to Earth? What materials were found in***

them? What's the biggest one, and where did it land? Did it cause any damage or hurt people?"

Great Grandpa smiled, his face lighting up at their enthusiasm. He leaned back in his chair, letting the moment linger before he spoke. "Ah, my little stargazers, what a fascinating question! Meteorites have indeed fallen to Earth, and each one brings with it a treasure trove of secrets from space. These cosmic visitors are made of many interesting materials—mostly iron and nickel, mixed with silicates, which are types of rock-forming minerals. Some even carry tiny traces of carbon and organic compounds, making scientists wonder if they hold clues about the origins of life itself."

He paused, letting the weight of his words settle. "Now, the largest meteorite ever found on Earth is called the *Hoba* meteorite. It lies in Namibia and weighs an astonishing 60 tons—that's as heavy as about ten elephants! It's made mostly of iron and nickel, and what's amazing is that it didn't create a crater when it landed. Scientists believe it must have slowed down significantly before hitting the ground."

The children gasped in awe, their imaginations running wild. Ibrahim piped up, "But **Great Grandpa**, *did any meteorites cause damage?"*

Great Grandpa nodded, his expression growing more serious. "Yes, there was an event in 1908, called the Tunguska event, in Siberia. A massive explosion, likely caused by a meteor or comet bursting in the air, flattened over 800 square miles of forest. Can you imagine that? Trees were knocked down like matchsticks! Luckily, it was in a remote area, so no one was harmed. But it was a powerful reminder of how mighty and unpredictable the universe can be."

He leaned forward, his voice soft yet filled with wonder. "Meteorites are like messengers from the heavens, carrying stories of distant worlds. They remind us how vast and connected the cosmos truly is. And every time one falls, it's as if the universe has written us a letter, waiting for us to read and understand it."

The **great-grandchildren** huddled close, whispering with a mix of mischief and relief, "Don't worry! The Creator of the universe has our backs—He'll make sure meteorites take a detour to forests or oceans. No crashing into our backyard anytime soon!"

Today's grandchildren are incredibly sharp-minded, always curious about the past and the future—thinking a century back and imagining a century ahead. Once again, they eagerly prepared a new set of thought-provoking questions.

"**Great Grandpa**, ***what are stars made of, and why do they shine? Are stars as big as the sun? Why do some stars look brighter than others? What are constellations, and how did they get their names? Can stars live forever, or do they eventually die?"***

For **Great Grandpa**, it was another challenging moment. But with a lifetime of wisdom, a century of experience, and a heart full of patience, he was ready to satisfy their curiosity. With his gentle words and thoughtful explanations, he turned their questions into a fascinating journey through the wonders of the universe, leaving his little ones captivated and eager to learn even more.

Great Grandpa smiled warmly. "Well, my little explorers, let's dive into the magic of the stars!"**What are stars made of, and why do they shine?** "Stars are made mostly of hydrogen and helium, which are types of gases. Deep inside them, there's something called nuclear fusion happening—like a giant fireworks show that never ends! This process releases an enormous amount of light and heat, which is why they shine so brightly. They're like giant cosmic light bulbs hanging in the universe!"

Are stars as big as the sun?

"Oh! Some stars are much bigger than the sun, while others are smaller. The sun is a medium-sized star, but because it's so close to us, it looks much bigger than the other stars in the sky."

Why do some stars look brighter than others?

"That's a great question! Some stars are closer to Earth, so they appear brighter. Others are naturally much bigger or hotter, which makes them shine more intensely. It's like comparing a flashlight to a big campfire—you'll notice the campfire from far away, but the flashlight has to be much closer for you to see it."

What are constellations, and how did they get their names?

"Ah, constellations are like connect-the-dots pictures in the sky. People long ago looked at the stars and imagined shapes—animals, people, or objects—and gave them names. Many of these names come from ancient Greek, Roman, and other myths and stories. For example, there's Orion, the hunter, and Ursa Major, the great bear. These constellations helped sailors navigate and inspired countless stories!"

Can stars live forever, or do they eventually die?

"Stars don't live forever, but their lifetimes are much longer than ours—millions or even billions of years! When a star uses up all its fuel, it changes. Small stars like our sun become beautiful clouds called nebulas and leave behind tiny stars called white dwarfs. Big stars end their lives with a bang—a supernova explosion! Some even become black holes, which are so powerful that not even light can escape them."

Great Grandpa paused, his voice filled with admiration for the universe. "You see, my dear ones, stars have their own life stories, just like us. They're born, they live, and eventually, they transform. And in their light, they remind us of the vast and beautiful universe we're a part of."

The children listened in awe, their imaginations now soaring across galaxies, eager to uncover more cosmic mysteries.

2. Planets and the Solar System

Mariyam, Ibrahim, and Yousuf ***were not ones to settle for simple answers; their boundless curiosity and sharp, inquisitive minds kept propelling them toward more cosmic mysteries. Even as Great Grandpa leaned back in his chair, savoring a brief moment of peace after the barrage of earlier questions, the children rallied once more, their eyes gleaming with excitement.***

"**Great Grandpa**!" **Mariyam** began, her voice brimming with enthusiasm. ***How many planets are there, and why do they stay in their orbits? Don't they ever want to float away?***

Ibrahim chimed in without skipping a beat, ***Which planet is the hottest? And which one is the coldest? Do they all feel the same way Earth does?***

Yousuf, always the dreamer, added his twist. ***Are there aliens living on other planets? Maybe some little green friends are waving at us right now!***

Before **Great Grandpa** could respond, **Mariyam** pressed on with another thought-provoking question, ***Why does Earth only have one moon, while other planets have so many? Is it because Earth is smaller or less special?***

Finally, **Ibrahim** posed the big one, his eyes sparkling with a mix of wonder and ambition. ***Do you think humans can ever live on Mars, Great Grandpa? Will we be able to build houses there and have our Martian adventures?***

Great Grandpa smiled, his weariness fading under the energy of their questions. He sat up straight, realizing that this wasn't just about answering their queries—it was about shaping their understanding of the universe and inspiring them to think even bigger.

"Well," he said, his voice rich with wisdom and warmth, "I suppose it's time for another journey through the cosmos, my little adventurers. Let's explore these mysteries together and uncover the secrets of our solar system and beyond!"

The room filled with eager anticipation as **Great Grandpa** prepared to answer, knowing that each word could spark a lifelong fascination with the wonders of the universe in the hearts of his great-grandchildren.

Ge leaned forward, his eyes twinkling with excitement as he began to respond.

"Well, **Mariyam**," he said, "there are eight planets (Mercury, Venus, Earth, Mars, Jupiter, Saturn, Uranus, and Neptune) in our solar system, and they stay in their orbits because of the Sun's gravity. It's like an invisible rope pulling them toward the Sun while their speed keeps them from falling straight into it. It's a perfect cosmic dance!"

Turning to Ibrahim, he added, "The hottest planet is Venus, even though Mercury is closer to the Sun. That's because Venus has a thick atmosphere that traps heat like a giant oven. As for the coldest, that would be Neptune, way out on the edge of the solar system, where it's freezing and dark in most of the areas."

Great Grandpa smiled at **Yousuf**'s question about aliens. "Ah, the idea of **aliens**! Scientists haven't found any proof of life on other planets yet, but the universe is so vast, with billions of stars and planets, that it's hard to believe we're the only ones here. Who knows? Maybe one day we'll find out!"

Looking back at **Mariyam**, he explained, "Earth has one moon because it formed that way after a big collision billions of years ago. Other planets, like Jupiter and Saturn, have many moons because they're much larger and have stronger gravity to capture all those moons over time."

Finally, he turned to **Ibrahim** with a thoughtful expression. **"Mars** has always fascinated humans. We've sent rovers and satellites to explore it, and there's even talk of people living there someday. But it's not easy—Mars is very cold, has very little air to breathe, and no liquid water on the surface. If humans ever live there, we'll need to build special habitats and bring supplies. It'll be like the ultimate camping trip, but on another planet!"

He leaned back with a chuckle. "The universe is full of mysteries, and I love seeing your curiosity light up the room. Keep asking questions, my little explorers. Who knows? One day, you might be the ones discovering the answers!" or "Will you be the daring astronauts of future manned missions to Mars or even the distant, mysterious Jupiter?"

For a moment, all three children fell silent, their curiosity ignited. They huddled together, whispering excitedly as they began crafting new questions. The air buzzed with their shared enthusiasm as they debated the mysteries of the universe.

Mysteries of the Moon, Aliens & Flying Saucers!

How was the moon formed? one of them pondered, eyes wide with wonder.

"What's the truth about aliens? Where could they be living, and where did they even come from?" another chimed in, her voice a mix of awe and anticipation.

"And what about flying saucers? Are they real? If so, who's behind them?"

They leaned in closer, their thoughts cascading into another question.

"And this Elon Musk...what's his big dream of settling humans on Mars all about? Can we live there?"

Their vibrant imagination turned the quiet room into a hub of cosmic exploration, as they eagerly awaited answers to the mysteries of worlds far beyond their reach.

Great Grandpa smiled warmly, his eyes twinkling as he leaned closer to the eager trio.

"Well, my dear little explorers," he began, his voice filled with a mix of wisdom and curiosity, "these are some fascinating questions! Let's explore them together, shall we?"

He pointed to the sky through the window. "The moon, for instance, is believed to have formed billions of years ago when a massive object collided with the young Earth. The debris from that collision eventually came together to create the beautiful moon we see today, lighting up our nights."

He paused, letting them picture the ancient celestial drama. "As for aliens, scientists are still searching for life beyond Earth. There are so many galaxies, planets, and stars out there that it's hard to believe we're completely alone. They might live on a faraway planet we've yet to discover."

Leaning in, he whispered conspiratorially, "Flying saucers? Those are often called UFOs—unidentified flying objects. Some people think they're visitors from other worlds. Others believe they're just advanced technology we don't fully understand yet. What do you think?"

Finally, he turned to the mission of Mars. "Ah, Elon Musk! He's a visionary who dreams of humans becoming a multi-planetary species. He's building powerful rockets to take people to Mars, where we could live in special habitats. Imagine playing on the red sands of Mars someday! Doesn't that sound incredible?"

His voice softened as he added, "What I love most about your questions is that they remind me of something very important—our universe is full of mysteries. And asking questions is how we begin to uncover them. Never stop wondering, my little stars. The answers you find might shape the world's future, or even the universe."

He leaned back with a satisfied smile, watching their eyes sparkle with imagination and wonder.

The little one, **Yousuf**, suddenly sprang to his feet, his eyes wide with excitement. "**Great Grandpa**," ***he exclaimed, his voice brimming with curiosity, "please tell us more about UFOs! Where have they been seen? Why haven't they been caught? Have scientists recorded what they do? And... is there a plan to deal with them in the future?"***

Great Grandpa chuckled, clearly delighted by the boy's enthusiasm. He leaned forward as if about to share a closely guarded secret.

"Well, **Yousuf** my dear, UFOs—Unidentified Flying Objects—have been spotted in many places around the world. People have seen strange lights moving quickly through the sky, objects hovering in ways that no airplane or helicopter can. Some sightings have been reported over deserts, mountains, and even the oceans. Isn't that fascinating?"

Yousuf nodded eagerly, his imagination taking flight.

"*As for why they haven't been 'caught,'*" **Great Grandpa** continued, his tone now mysterious, "that's because these objects are often so fast and elusive. They move in ways our current technology can't keep up with. Sometimes, they appear for just a few seconds before vanishing completely! It's like they're playing hide-and-seek with us."

His voice dropped to a softer, more serious tone. "And yes, scientists and even military organizations have recorded some of these incidents. There are videos and radar data showing objects moving at incredible speeds or making sharp turns that no human-made vehicle could manage. Governments have declassified some of these reports in recent years, but much of it remains a mystery."

Yousuf's jaw dropped. "Really? ***What are they doing about it?***"

Great Grandpa smiled knowingly. "Ah, that's the big question, isn't it? Scientists are working hard to study these phenomena. They've even created special programs to analyze the sightings and figure out if they're natural occurrences, advanced technology from another country, or something truly extraordinary—maybe even from another world!"

He paused, his voice becoming thoughtful. "The plan? Well, it's all about gathering more evidence, improving our technology to track these objects, and perhaps one day... making contact. But here's the most exciting part, **Yousuf**—every question we ask about UFOs brings us closer to unlocking the secrets of our universe. Who knows? Maybe one day, you'll be the scientist solving these mysteries!"

Yousuf's eyes sparkled with wonder as he sat back down, lost in thoughts of far-off worlds and mysterious visitors.

Great Grandpa's face lit up with a gentle smile, the kind that carried the weight of years and the warmth of boundless love. His words, wrapped in the charm of both wisdom and affection, seemed to weave a spell around the children, leaving them yearning for more. Their curiosity was unstoppable, a spark of wonder igniting a cascade of new questions about the endless mysteries of the sky. After all, they were children of the 21st century, born into an era of limitless imagination and discovery.

Leaning in, their eager faces alight with anticipation, it was **Mariyam** who broke the silence. Her voice, soft yet brimming with excitement, carried the innocence of a child and the thirst of a budding explorer. "**Great Grandpa**," she began, her wide eyes shimmering like the very stars they spoke of, ***"why does the moon change shape every night? Is it... is it playing hide-and-seek with us?"***

Great Grandpa chuckled, his laughter a gentle ripple in the room, as he prepared to unravel another celestial mystery for his wide-eyed audience.

Ibrahim chimed in, his voice filled with intrigue, ***"And what about those dark spots on the moon? Are they shadows, or something else entirely?"***

Little **Yousuf**, always drawn to fantastical tales, added with excitement, ***"Is there a man on the moon, like the stories Mama tells us? Does he live there all alone?"***

Before **Great Grandpa** could respond, **Mariyam** pressed further, her voice a mix of amazement and disbelief, "**Great Grandpa**, ***have people walked on the moon? What was it like for them?"***

The room seemed to come alive with their questions, each one more animated than the last. Great Grandpa smiled warmly, his white beard catching the golden rays of sunlight filtering through the curtains. He took a deep breath, ready to transport his inquisitive little stars into the captivating world of celestial wonders once again.

Great Grandpa adjusted his glasses, leaned back in his armchair, and smiled warmly at his eager audience. "Ah, my little explorers," he began, "let's uncover the moon's secrets together."

Looking at **Mariyam**, he said, "The moon doesn't change shape every night, my dear. What we see is the moon reflecting sunlight, and its shape depends on how much of it is lit up as it orbits the Earth. We call these changing shapes the 'phases of the moon.' It's like a dance between the sun, the Earth, and the moon—sometimes we see a lot of light, like during a full moon, and sometimes just a sliver, like a crescent moon."

Turning to **Ibrahim**, he continued, "And those dark spots on the moon? They're called 'maria,' which means seas in Latin, but don't be fooled—there's no water there. They're vast plains of ancient lava that cooled down billions of years ago. They give the moon its unique look, almost like a face smiling back at us."

Little **Yousuf**'s question made him chuckle. "A man on the moon, you say? Well, that's a story people have loved to tell for generations. Some see the dark spots and imagine a man, others see a rabbit or even a woman weaving on a loom. But no, my boy, no man is living on the moon—it's a cold, silent world."

Then he turned to **Mariyam**'s last question, his tone growing more serious. “Yes, people have walked on the moon! The first were astronauts Neil Armstrong and Buzz Aldrin in 1969. They flew on a spacecraft called Apollo 11. Imagine this: they stepped onto the moon's dusty surface and looked up to see the Earth glowing in the sky—a tiny blue marble in the vastness of space. It was one of humanity's greatest achievements.”

With a twinkle in his eye and a voice rich with nostalgia, **Great Grandpa** leaned in closer to his wide-eyed audience. “The moon,” he began, “has been our steadfast companion for millions of years, silently watching over us as we journey through time. It has inspired countless tales and timeless verses in literature across the globe. Here in the subcontinent, it has woven its magic into the soulful tapestry of Urdu poetry and ghazals, where lovers pour out their hearts beneath its gentle glow.”

His gaze drifted upward as if he could see the moon's silvery light filtering through the room. “It has been a muse for dreamers and poets, lighting the path for those who dared to imagine the impossible. And now, it's inspiring you—your questions, your curiosity, your dreams. That fills my heart with a joy I can hardly put into words.”

He paused, letting the weight of his words sink in, before continuing with a playful smile. “Who knows? With the way technology is advancing, you might one day pack your picnic baskets, hop onto a rocket, and spend an unforgettable day basking in the moon's serene glow. You'll eat, laugh, and play under its ancient craters, only to return home by nightfall, just in time to watch the stars sparkle over Earth's skies,” and kids' computer cartoons back home.

Great Grandpa's voice softened as he placed a loving hand on **Maryam**, **Ibrahim**, and **Yousuf**'s shoulders. “I may not live to see that day, my dear ones. But I do not doubt that you will. You'll be the pioneers of that incredible future, and I'll be watching from the heavens, so proud of the wonders you'll achieve.”

The room fell silent, the children's imaginations soaring as they envisioned a future filled with moonlit adventures, all while their great-grandpa's words echoed warmly in their hearts.

By this time, **Great Grandpa** let out a soft sigh, his warm smile giving way to a hint of weariness. "Well, my little adventurers," he said, adjusting his glasses, "it seems even great storytellers need a break to recharge. It's time for me to enjoy a hearty lunch and take a short afternoon nap to gather my energy for our next session."

The children, sensing his tiredness but still brimming with excitement, exchanged glances and nodded in agreement. "Alright, **Great Grandpa**," **Yousuf** said with a grin. "We'll have our lunch too and take a rest so we're ready for more stories and questions in the evening!"

Great Grandpa chuckled. "That's the spirit! A little rest will make our second session even more magical." With that, they parted ways, each anticipating the delightful adventures that awaited them when they reconvened later in the day.

3. Space Exploration

For the second round of their ever-curious questionnaire, the great-grandchildren were brimming with excitement. Their eyes sparkled with anticipation, their young minds teeming with new thoughts and boundless imagination. It was as though their curiosity had a life of its own, always urging them to think beyond the ordinary, to explore new realms of wonder.

Perhaps it was the influence of the colorful, futuristic cartoons they adored, where robots talked and spaceships zoomed across galaxies. Or maybe it was the fantastical stories they devoured in their favorite books, where brave adventurers journeyed to unknown planets. Add to this the magical bedtime tales spun by Ma and Grandma under the vast open sky, with the stars twinkling as if nodding in agreement—it was no wonder their minds were always racing with questions and ideas.

On the other side of this lively scene sat **Great Grandpa**, a calm yet formidable figure, fully prepared to meet their thirst for knowledge head-on. His wisdom, sharpened by decades of learning and experience, was now complemented by his fascination with modern discoveries. **Great Grandpa** wasn't just a keeper of old stories—he was a seeker of new knowledge.

He spent hours immersed in the latest scientific journals, devouring articles on space exploration, the mysteries of black holes, and the astonishing feats of technology that were transforming human understanding of the cosmos. From the first steps on the Moon to the ambitious plans for Mars colonization, **Great Grandpa** kept himself updated on the cutting-edge advancements of this dynamic 21st century.

His vast reservoir of knowledge wasn't just for himself—it was a gift he loved sharing with his inquisitive great-grandchildren. Their endless questions energized him, their imaginations inspired him, and their eagerness to learn filled him with a deep sense of purpose.

As they gathered once more, their tiny faces alight with expectation, **Great Grandpa** smiled, his heart warmed by the sight. "Alright, my little adventurers," he said, his voice filled with playful authority. "What new mysteries of the universe shall we uncover today?"

The children leaned in closer, their imaginations soaring beyond the room, ready to embark on another journey guided by their great-grandpa's timeless wisdom and ever-expanding knowledge. This was not just a conversation—it was a shared adventure across the infinite wonders of the cosmos.

Maryam's Exciting Questions:

Being the eldest, **Mariyam** took the lead with her sparkling eyes and an eager smile. "**Great Grandpa**," she began, ***"how do rockets and spaceships travel to space? And what's NASA's role in all this? What's it like being an astronaut? How do they sleep and eat in space? Oh, and have scientists ever found life on another planet? If we do, can I send gifts like Barbie dolls to my girlfriend over there? And, what's the farthest place humans have traveled in space?"***

Great Grandpa's Response:

Great Grandpa chuckled, his eyes twinkling with delight at **Mariyam**'s imaginative flair. "Ah, **Mariyam**, your questions are as vast as the universe itself!" he began. "Let's take it step by step. Rockets and spaceships use powerful engines called rocket boosters to escape Earth's gravity. Think of it like a super-strong push that helps them break free from our planet and reach outer space."

"As for NASA, they're like the maestros of space exploration, planning missions, designing spacecraft, and training astronauts to explore the unknown. And speaking of astronauts—they're some of the bravest people alive! They float around in zero gravity, sleep in special sleeping bags that keep them from drifting, and eat food packed in small pouches. Imagine drinking juice from a straw while it floats in mid-air!"

He leaned in with a twinkle in his eye and a playful grin. "Ah, sending Barbie dolls to your alien girlfriend, are we? Well, scientists are still on the hunt for life beyond Earth. They're exploring planets like Mars and icy moons like Europa, where water—our essential ingredient for life—might exist. But as far as pen pals from another galaxy go, I'm sorry to say, no alien addresses have turned up just yet. Maybe you'll be the one to make that historic discovery!"

"The farthest place humans have traveled is the Moon. The Apollo astronauts walked there, and who knows? Maybe one day, you'll be part of a team that travels even farther!"

Ibrahim's Brilliant Brainstorm:

Not to be outdone, **Ibrahim** chimed in, his forehead furrowed in thought. "**Great Grandpa**, ***what are satellites, and how do they help us? What's the farthest place humans have traveled in space? Are there other galaxies like ours? How big is the universe, and does it ever end?"***

Great Grandpa's Response:

Great Grandpa tapped his chin thoughtfully. "Satellites are like helpful spies or assistants in the sky! They orbit Earth and do all sorts of things—helping us predict the weather, connecting our phones, guiding ships, and even taking pictures of space to help scientists learn more about the universe."

As for other galaxies, oh yes! There are billions of them, each with millions or even billions of stars, just like our own Milky Way. The universe is mind-blowingly vast—it's so big that we can't even measure it fully. And does it end? That's one of the biggest mysteries. Scientists think it's still expanding like a balloon being blown up, so the edge is always moving farther away!

Yousuf's Cute Curiosity:

Little **Yousuf,** determined not to be left behind, raised his tiny hand and asked, **Great Grandpa**, ***what are black holes? Do they suck everything in? What's the Milky Way, and can we see it from here? What happens during an eclipse? Why is space so dark if there are so many stars? Can we ever touch a star or visit one? And why does***

Earth have gravity, but space doesn't? Oh, and if I had a telescope, could I see other planets or galaxies from my room?

Great Grandpa's Response:

Great Grandpa chuckled heartily, pulling Yousuf into a snug embrace. "**Yousuf**, my little wonder, you're a treasure chest of questions! Your curiosity could make even the smartest minds in the universe stop and think!" His eyes sparkled with affection as he continued, "Alright, let's dive into this cosmic adventure together. Black holes are like invisible whirlpools in space, pulling in everything around them with gravity so strong that not even light can escape. But don't worry," he added with a playful grin, "the nearest black hole is thousands of light-years away—plenty of room to keep us safe and sound!"

Then, **Great Grandpa** leaned in conspiratorially and asked, "Do you know what a light-year is, my darling?" Without waiting, he began to explain, "It's not about time, like days or years; it's about distance. A light-year is how far light can travel in a single year. And light is incredibly fast—it races through space at 300,000 kilometers per second. That means in one year, it travels nearly 9.46 trillion kilometers! Isn't that incredible? It's like having a ruler made entirely of light to measure the vastness of the universe."

He paused, letting the wonder sink in as Yousuf's eyes grew wide with amazement. "So, when we say a star or black hole is a thousand light-years away, we mean the light we see today started its journey to us a thousand years ago. It's like peeking into the past every time we look at the night sky!"

Yousuf nodded slowly, his curiosity ablaze. "Wow, **Great Grandpa**," he murmured, "it's like magic!"

Great Grandpa leaned back slightly, his voice taking on a tone of awe. "And here's where it gets even more fascinating. Black holes are born when giant stars come to the end of their lives. They collapse under their weight, squeezing all their mass into a tiny, infinitely dense point called a singularity. Around this singularity is a boundary we call the event horizon.

Once anything crosses that line—a star, a planet, or even light itself—it's gone forever, pulled into the black hole's depths."

The children sat riveted, their imaginations soaring. **Great Grandpa**'s voice grew more animated. "But the real mystery of black holes? Scientists think they might hold clues to how the universe works. Could they be gateways to other dimensions? Could they teach us how time and space bend and twist? No one knows for sure. That's why they're so exciting to study!"

With a playful gleam in his eye, he leaned closer and said, "And who knows? Maybe one of you will grow up to be the astronaut who solves the riddle of black holes. Can you imagine that? **Yousuf**, **Mariyam**, or **Ibrahim**—the explorer who unlocks the secrets of the cosmos!"

The children gasped, their young minds alive with possibilities. The vast, mysterious universe suddenly felt a little closer, brimming with wonder and waiting to be explored.

"The Milky Way is our galaxy, a massive collection of stars, planets, and space dust. On a clear night far from city lights, you can see it as a hazy band stretching across the sky. It's breathtaking!"

"During a solar eclipse, the Moon passes between the Sun and Earth, blocking the Sun's light. In a lunar eclipse, Earth gets between the Sun and Moon, casting a shadow on the Moon. It's like a cosmic game of hide-and-seek!"

"Now, space is dark because, unlike Earth, it has no atmosphere to scatter sunlight. And as for touching a star—oh, I wish we could! But stars are fiery balls of gas, burning millions of miles away. They're too far and too hot for a visit. But through a telescope, you can see planets, moons, and even other galaxies right from your room. Isn't that amazing?"

He ended with a wink. "And Earth has gravity because it's big enough to pull everything towards it. Space doesn't have gravity because there's nothing big nearby to create that pull. But who knows, Yousuf? Maybe one day you'll discover something new about gravity!"

The children giggled, their imaginations soaring as they pictured black holes, fiery stars, and their telescopes uncovering the mysteries of the cosmos. Great Grandpa's stories awakened them, eager for more adventures into the infinite universe.

As the sun dipped below the horizon, painting the sky with hues of amber and crimson, the lively conversation between Great-Grandpa and his great-grandchildren seemed to reach a natural pause. But just as the laughter began to fade and the children started to stretch and yawn, **Great Grandpa** leaned back in his chair, his eyes gleaming with a mischievous spark.

"Well," he began, his voice carrying the weight of mystery, "there is something I've never told anyone before. A story so peculiar, so extraordinary, that even I sometimes wonder if it was a dream..."

The great-grandchildren instantly perked up, their sleepiness forgotten. Clutching his stuffed rocket, **Yousuf** whispered, "What is it, **Great Grandpa**? Tell us!" **Mariyam** and **Ibrahim** scooted closer, their eyes wide with curiosity, hanging on his every word.

Great Grandpa stroked his beard thoughtfully, drawing out the suspense. "It's about the night I saw something in the sky—something I couldn't explain. A flash of light, brighter than the moon, danced across the heavens before disappearing into the stars. It wasn't a plane, and it wasn't a shooting star. What it was...I'll leave you to decide."

"*Was it a UFO? Did aliens visit you*?" Ibrahim gasped.

"Or ***was it a secret spacecraft?***" **Mariyam** added, her mind racing.

"The adorable **Yousuf**, with wide, innocent eyes and a mischievous grin, exclaimed, '**Great Grandpa**, watch out—it must have been a heavenly ghost coming down to give you a little scare!"

All three children burst into uncontrollable laughter, their giggles echoing through the room like a chorus of pure joy, their faces lighting up with sheer delight as they playfully teased great-grandpa.

Great Grandpa chuckled, his voice tinged with both amusement and intrigue. "That's a tale for another day, my curious explorers. For now, let's leave it to your imagination. After all, some mysteries are better left unsolved—for a little while, at least."

The children groaned in unison, pleading for more, but **Great Grandpa** simply smiled, a knowing look in his eyes. "Tomorrow," he promised, "we'll unravel more of the universe's secrets. But tonight, dream of the stars and let your imaginations take you where even I cannot."

As he rose from his chair and bid them goodnight, the **great-grandchildren** exchanged eager whispers, their minds buzzing with possibilities. What could **Great Grandpa**'s mysterious story mean? The promise of another thrilling session hung in the air, leaving them—and the readers—eagerly awaiting the next chapter in this enchanting tale of wisdom, wonder, and the boundless curiosity of young hearts.

Session Three

Timeless Tales: Exploring Fact and Fiction Across Generations

A Morning of Merriment and Curiosity

As the sun cast its gentle rays over the backyard garden, a cool breeze whispered through the air, setting the stage for the third session of conversations between **Great-Grandpa** and his **great-grandchildren**. The children, having relished their breakfast, now nibbled on salted roasted pistachios hidden in their pockets, their laughter mingling with the chirping of birds.

In the heart of the garden, they settled upon a vibrant Egyptian carpet, its intricate patterns of blue, red, and yellow weaving a tapestry that mirrored the surrounding beauty. The air was alive with color and movement: flowers in full bloom beckoned butterflies to dance above them, while nearby, apple and persimmon trees stood heavy with ripe, red fruit. Opposite, pear trees extended their branches, offering a bountiful harvest. An automatic sprinkler system cast shimmering droplets over the flora, enhancing the enchanting atmosphere. Among the branches, colorful birds chirped melodiously, savoring the sweet juices of the persimmons, while hummingbirds flitted to and from their nests. In the distance, drones from courier services buzzed as they delivered packages to nearby homes, and executives from various IT companies commuted through the low-flying airspace to their offices. It was a harmonious blend of nature and technology, coexisting seamlessly in this serene setting.

Great Grandpa, having completed his peaceful morning rituals, sat back with a serene smile, the aroma of freshly brewed black coffee curling around him like an old friend. He looked utterly content, his eyes twinkling with warmth as they rested on the vibrant bouquet lovingly crafted by his **great-grandchildren**. Each flower seemed to whisper a tale of love and innocence. The atmosphere was just right—calm yet buzzing with the quiet excitement of curious minds ready to explore. With hearts refreshed and spirits high, they gathered around him once again. The stage was perfectly set for another enchanting session of questions, stories, and laughter. It was going to be one of those unforgettable days—woven with wonder, wisdom, and the timeless magic of togetherness.

Futuristic Travel:

Maryam, the eldest, leaned forward with a sparkle in her eyes. "**Great Grandpa**," she began, ***"imagine if we could travel across the vast Atlantic and Pacific Oceans in supersonic trains, zooming faster than the speed of sound! What would such a journey feel like?"*** The other children edged closer, their excitement palpable. "And picture this," **Maryam** continued, ***"floating stations anchored amidst the tumultuous seas, standing firm against storms and towering waves. Could trains navigate through the enigmatic Bermuda Triangle without a hitch?" Their faces lit up with wonder, each envisioning a future brimming with thrilling adventures and groundbreaking innovations.***

Ibrahim, with a mischievous grin, chimed in, "**Great Grandpa**, ***what about building trains that travel underwater across the oceans? Wouldn't that make transportation more affordable and safer?***" His laughter was infectious, and soon everyone was giggling at the thought of submarines doubling as passenger trains.

Little **Yousuf**, not wanting to be left out, waited patiently for his turn. "**Great Grandpa**," ***he said earnestly, "what if we had floating or hanging airports on the surfaces of the Atlantic and Pacific Oceans? But let's avoid the Bermuda area; I've heard that powerful ghosts have their villas there. They must be more advanced than us because they can destroy even the strongest ships and aircraft that cross their path!"*** *His innocent expression mixed with the fantastical notion had* *everyone chuckling, adding a touch of whimsy to their imaginative discussion.*

Great Grandpa chuckled, his eyes twinkling with amusement as he listened to Mariaym's imaginative questions. "Ah, **Mariaym**," he began, "the idea of soaring across the vast Atlantic and Pacific Oceans in supersonic trains, speeding faster than sound, is indeed a thrilling one! Visionaries like Elon Musk have proposed concepts such as a transatlantic tunnel utilizing hyperloop technology, which could potentially transport passengers between London and New York in under an hour. This ambitious project, estimated to cost around $20 trillion (an amount equivalent to the GDP of the United States), would involve constructing a vacuum-sealed tunnel beneath the ocean, allowing pressurized vehicles to travel at speeds up to 3,000 mph.

"As for floating stations amid raging seas, unshaken by storms and waves," **Great Grandpa** continued, "the concept of floating airports has been around for many years. While no long-term functioning airport has yet been built, the potential technological and economic feasibility of such structures has been examined.

These floating airports would be designed to withstand harsh ocean conditions, providing stable platforms for aircraft operations.

Turning to **Ibrahim**, **Great Grandpa** smiled warmly. "Building an underwater train in the oceans to make transport cheaper and safer is a fascinating idea. There have been proposals for underwater hyperloop systems that could revolutionize cargo transport. For instance, Hyperloop One has expressed interest in developing an underwater version of its system to move cargo to floating ports located 10 miles offshore.

Such innovations could potentially reduce transportation costs and improve safety by providing direct and rapid transit routes beneath the ocean's surface.

Finally, addressing little **Yousuf's** concern about floating or hanging airports on the surface of the Atlantic and Pacific Oceans, Great Grandpa chuckled softly. "The Bermuda Triangle has long been the subject of myths and legends, with tales of powerful ghosts making their villas there and causing ships and aircraft to disappear. However, scientific investigations have not found any evidence to support these claims. The challenges of constructing floating airports in such regions are more related to engineering and environmental factors than supernatural ones. With advancements in technology, building stable and safe floating airports is becoming more feasible, allowing us to overcome the mysteries of the deep with innovation and ingenuity."

The children erupted into giggles at the whimsical notion of ghostly villas in the Bermuda Triangle, their imaginations painting vivid pictures of spectral neighbors hosting eerie soirées. Great Grandpa's tales not only quenched their thirst for knowledge but also filled the room with laughter and wonder, sketching a future where such extraordinary ideas might just leap from fantasy to reality.

Yet, despite the jovial atmosphere, **Yousuf** couldn't shake his apprehension. The thought of tampering with the Bermuda Triangle sent shivers down his spine. ***"What if," he mused, "disturbing that mysterious zone causes those enigmatic forces to pack up their ghostly bags and move into our peaceful neighborhood?"*** The mere idea of spectral beings setting up residence next door made **Yousuf** even more cautious about venturing into the Triangle's enigmatic domain.

As the sun began its ascent, casting a warm glow over the garden, everyone started to feel a bit tired and in need of a break. **Great Grandpa** suggested taking some time to relax. He lay down, resting his head on a soft plllow, and opened the day's newspaper to catch up on current events, including the recent inauguration of President Donald Trump and his notable address to the nation. Meanwhile, the children picked up their badminton rackets and began an energetic game, their laughter filling the backyard as the shuttlecock flew back and forth.

As time passed, the sun's rays became more intense, and the increasing heat made everyone a bit uncomfortable. Noticing this, **Maryam** suggested, *"Why don't we move inside to the family room?* ***Great Grandpa*** *can relax in his favorite armchair, and we can continue our conversation there."* The idea was met with enthusiasm, and soon they all gathered in the cool comfort of the family room, ready to resume their engaging discussions.

As everyone settled comfortably, the children eagerly prepared to delve into **Great Grandpa's** past. They were excited to ask him about his childhood adventures, the stories of his upbringing, and the experiences that shaped his life. Their minds buzzed with questions, ready to uncover the rich tapestry of **Great Grandpa**'s history.

The Little Interviewers: Digging into Great Grandpa's Life:

As the family gathered in the cozy family room, **Ibrahim** hesitated for a moment before speaking up. "**Great Grandpa**, ***would you mind if we asked you some personal questions?***"

Great Grandpa smiled warmly and nodded. "Of course not, **Ibrahim**, my young friend. Go ahead."

Ibrahim took a deep breath and began, ***"What is your earliest childhood memory, and how has it influenced your life?"***

Great Grandpa leaned back, his eyes twinkling with nostalgia. "I remember being about five years old, helping my father plant a small tree in our backyard. He told me that with care and patience, it would grow tall and strong, just like I would. That lesson taught me the value of nurturing and perseverance, which has guided me throughout my life."

Encouraged, **Ibrahim** continued, ***"Can you share a pivotal moment in your life that shaped you?***"

Great Grandpa nodded thoughtfully. "When I was a young man, I moved to a new city for work. It was challenging, but it taught me resilience and the importance of stepping out of my comfort zone. That experience shaped my confidence and adaptability."

Ibrahim asked, ***"What lessons have you learned from overcoming challenges, and how can they guide us?"***

Great Grandpa replied, "I've learned that every challenge carries a lesson. Facing difficulties head-on builds strength and character. Remember, it's okay to stumble, but always get back up and keep moving forward."

Ibrahim's final question was, ***"How did people maintain long-lasting friendships and relationships when you were my age?"***

Great Grandpa smiled. "We valued face-to-face interactions and made efforts to stay connected, even without today's technology. Writing letters, visiting friends, and spending quality time together was key to maintaining strong bonds."

Next, **Yousuf** stepped forward. ***"Great Grandpa, how did technological advancements during your youth compare to today's innovations?***"

Great Grandpa chuckled. "When I was young, the most exciting technology was the introduction of black and white television. Compared to today's smartphones and the internet, it seems simple, but back then, it was revolutionary."

Maryam, her eyes sparkling with curiosity, couldn't contain herself and asked, ***"Great Grandpa, we've come a long way from black-and-white TVs to today's smart digital ones. Do you think we'll ever be able to smell flowers through our TVs?"***

Great Grandpa chuckled softly, appreciating her inquisitiveness. "That's a fascinating question, **Maryam.** In fact, scientists have been exploring this idea for some time. Researchers at the University of California, San

Diego, in collaboration with Samsung, have developed a compact device capable of generating thousands of different scents. This device is small enough to attach to the back of a TV, allowing viewers to experience various smells corresponding to the on-screen content."

He continued, "Additionally, companies have introduced accessories like MovieScent, which releases fragrances to match what's happening on the screen. For instance, during a beach scene, you might smell the ocean."

"While these technologies are still in development and not yet widespread," **Great Grandpa** added, "the progress is promising. So, it's quite possible that in the future, you'll be able to enjoy the scent of flowers blooming right from your TV screen."

Maryam's face lit up with excitement at the thought of such immersive experiences becoming a reality.

Yousuf asked, ***"What significant world events do you recall, and how did they impact your community?***"

Great Grandpa's expression grew serious. "I remember the moon landing in 1969. It filled us with awe and a sense of unity, showing that humanity could achieve incredible feats."

Yousuf continued, ***"Are there any family traditions or stories passed down through generations that you'd like us to continue?"***

Great Grandpa nodded. "Our annual family reunion picnic is a tradition I'd love for you to continue. It keeps our family close and allows us to share stories and create memories."

Yousuf's last question was, ***"Were you named after a family member, or does your name have a special meaning?"***

Great Grandpa smiled. "I was named after my grandfather, a man known for his wisdom and kindness. I've always strived to live up to his legacy."

Finally, **Mariyam** asked, ***"If you could witness one future technological advancement, what would it be?"***

Great Grandpa's eyes sparkled. "I'd love to see a cure for all diseases, bringing health and longevity to everyone."

Maryam continued, ***"How do you envision the world changing in the next 50 years?***"

Great Grandpa pondered. "I imagine a world more connected, with advancements in technology making life easier, but also hope we don't lose the personal touch in our relationships."

Mariyam asked, ***"If you could travel back in time, is there anything you would do differently?***"

Great Grandpa shook his head gently. "Every choice I made, right or wrong, taught me something valuable. I wouldn't change a thing."

Maryam's final question was, ***"What hobbies or activities have brought you the most joy throughout your life?"***

Great Grandpa smiled warmly. "Gardening has always been my passion. Watching something grow and flourish brings me immense joy."

The room was filled with a sense of connection and understanding as **Great Grandpa** shared his stories, leaving the grandchildren with valuable lessons and cherished memories.

The children, eyes wide with curiosity, asked in unison, "**Great Grandpa**, do you think we can contribute to technology in a way that helps the world where It's needed most?"

Great Grandpa smiled warmly, appreciating their eagerness. "My dear ones," he began. "There are several areas where your future innovations could make a significant impact."

1. Clean Energy Solutions: "Developing technologies that provide affordable and sustainable energy is crucial. Innovations in renewable energy sources, like solar and wind power, can help reduce our reliance on fossil fuels and combat climate change."

2. Access to Clean Water: "Creating efficient water purification systems can ensure that communities around the world have access to safe drinking water. This is a pressing need in many regions."

3. Healthcare Accessibility: "Advancements in telemedicine and portable medical devices can bring healthcare services to remote and underserved areas, improving the quality of life for many."

4. Education Technology: "Developing educational tools and platforms can provide learning opportunities to children worldwide, regardless of their location or economic status."

5. Environmental Conservation: "Innovations in technology can aid in monitoring and protecting our environment, helping to preserve biodiversity and natural resources for future generations."

He concluded, "By focusing on these areas, you can use technology to address some of the world's most pressing challenges. Remember, meaningful change often starts with a simple idea and a passion to make a difference."

The children nodded thoughtfully, inspired by **Great Grandpa**'s words and eager to explore how they could contribute to a better future.

The **great-grandchildren**, eyes wide with curiosity, gathered around Great Grandpa. Unable to contain their excitement, they asked in unison, "**Great Grandpa**, we know that Elon Musk is a visionary entrepreneur whose contributions span multiple technological domains, each aimed at advancing human capabilities and addressing global challenges, including Space Exploration and Mars Colonization, Electric Vehicles and Sustainable Energy, Hyperloop and Transportation Innovation, Neuralink and Brain-Computer Interfaces, The Boring Company and Infrastructure, and Artificial Intelligence and OpenAI. Do you think we can contribute to these innovations and be part of his noble mission?"

Great Grandpa leaned back in his favorite armchair, a thoughtful smile spreading across his face. "My dear ones," he began, "Elon Musk himself has often shared advice for young people like you. He encourages you to 'try to be useful' and to 'contribute more than you consume.' This means focusing on how you can make a positive impact on society."

He continued, "Musk also suggests that young people should 'learn as much as possible' and 'read a lot of books.' By gaining knowledge, especially in areas like physics, you can develop the skills needed to contribute to technological advancements."

Great Grandpa's eyes twinkled as he added, "Remember, meaningful contributions often start with a simple idea and a passion to make a difference. By focusing on being useful and continuously learning, you can find ways to be part of innovations that benefit the world."

The children nodded eagerly, inspired by Great Grandpa's words and excited about the possibilities that lay ahead.

As the sun dipped below the horizon, it painted the sky with shades of orange and pink. Shadows grew longer, and the first stars began to twinkle. Birds chirped softly as they flew back to their nests, adding to the calm of the evening. **Great Grandpa** decided it was the perfect time for his evening walk to the nearby community garden. He suggested the children take a break for some snacks and then start their homework. With smiles and nods, they all agreed, bringing their wonderful day to a gentle close.

Dear readers, we're excited to announce that the fourth session of our conversations with **Great Grandpa** and his great-grandchildren is scheduled for next weekend, once the children have completed their homework. In the meantime, take care of your health, and stay happy, and we look forward to sharing more engaging stories and ideas with you soon.

Session Four

Echoes of Tomorrow: A Great-Grandfather's Conversations with the Next Generation

Great Grandpa and the Kids' Adventure into AI and Robotics

The children had stayed up late the previous night finishing their homework, so they slept in this morning. Despite the late start, they appeared relaxed and comfortable. **Great Grandpa**, as per his routine, had risen early, completed his morning walk, and was now savoring his coffee. The morning was particularly pleasant, with comfortably cool weather, a gentle breeze, and a drizzle beginning to fall. **Great Grandpa** eagerly awaited the children's arrival, contemplating the venue for their conversation but leaving the choice to them.

The youngest, **Yousuf**, was the first to come downstairs. He greeted **Great Grandpa** warmly and received a loving embrace in return, finding a cozy spot on his lap. **Great Grandpa's** eyes sparkled with joy at **Yousuf's** presence. Soon after, **Maryam** and **Ibrahim** joined them in the family room. Noticing **Yousuf** comfortably seated on **Great Grandpa**'s lap, they felt a twinge of envy but were quickly reassured by his warm greetings and handshakes. They settled on the carpet near his armchair, ready to begin.

Great-Grandpa inquired if they had eaten breakfast. When they shook their heads, he gently urged them to have their meal first and then reconvene to decide on the conversation's location. The children nodded and headed to the kitchen.

After finishing their breakfast, the trio returned, looking refreshed and eager. The family room buzzed with their lively chatter and laughter, bringing a vibrant energy to the space. **Great Grandpa**, energized by their enthusiasm, felt a youthful spirit himself. The children playfully surrounded his armchair, showering him with compliments on his youthful appearance. It was a beautiful gathering, a harmonious blend of past and future. In today's fast-paced society, such intergenerational connections are rare yet invaluable. Spending quality time with elders allows children to learn about their heritage and family traditions, fostering a greater understanding between generations.

Moreover, these interactions can combat social isolation and improve health, easing fears associated with aging.In a world where everyone seems busy and the future uncertain, moments like these, filled with wisdom and compassion, are truly precious.

When **Great Grandpa** asked where they would like to have their conversation, the children exchanged ideas. Considering the ongoing drizzle outside, they unanimously chose to stay in the cozy family room. With the decision made, they settled in, ready for another engaging session of stories and discussions with their beloved great-grandpa.

As the long-awaited question round commenced, **Maryam** took the lead with a curious glint in her eye. She began, "**Great Grandpa**, ***what exactly defines a robot, and how do they perceive and interact with the world around them?"***

Great Grandpa chuckled softly, "Ah, **Maryam**, imagine a robot as a mechanical helper, designed to perform tasks, sometimes tirelessly, without needing a nap or a cookie break! They perceive their surroundings using sensors—like our eyes and ears—that gather information. This data is processed by their 'brains,' or control systems, allowing them to respond appropriately. For instance, some robots use cameras to see and touch sensors to feel, helping them navigate and interact with objects."

Intrigued, **Maryam** continued, ***"Can you tell us how robots are assisting in medical surgeries today, and what advancements we might see in the future to improve patient care?"***

Nodding, **Great Grandpa** replied, "Certainly! Today, robots are like skilled surgical assistants. They help doctors perform delicate procedures with high precision, often through tiny incisions, which means less pain and quicker recovery for patients. For example, robotic systems are used in urology and gynecology surgeries, providing enhanced control and accuracy. Looking ahead, we might see even smaller robots, perhaps micro-robots, that can navigate the body to perform intricate tasks, making surgeries less invasive and more efficient."

Eager to delve deeper, **Maryam** asked, ***"How have robots contributed to space missions so far, and what roles might they play in future explorations of distant planets?"***

With a twinkle in his eye, **Great Grandpa** answered, "Ah, space—the final frontier! Robots have been our trailblazers, venturing where humans couldn't. Robotic rovers like those on Mars have been exploring the terrain, conducting experiments, and sending valuable data back to Earth. In the future, we can expect robots to set up habitats, mine resources, and perhaps even prepare planets for human arrival. They'll be our cosmic construction workers and explorers, paving the way for human footsteps."

The great-grandchildren listened intently, their imaginations ignited by the fascinating possibilities **Great Grandpa** painted with his words.

Maryam, with her sharp wit and sparkling eyes, leaned forward as if she had uncovered a treasure trove of possibilities. "**Great Grandpa**," she began, her voice brimming with excitement, ***"does this mean future robots can be very useful? Like... super useful! They'll work as housemaids who come on time and leave on time. They won't lie, won't make excuses like 'traffic congestion,' won't waste time napping, and—most importantly—won't secretly eat our cookies and chocolates!"***

She giggled at the thought, then added, ***"And they'll give you your blood pressure and diabetes medicines right on time, along with your favorite coffee in the morning and fresh orange juice during***

breakfast. Isn't that amazing? They could even prepare our dresses, pack our tiffins, arrange our school bags—especially for Yousuf and Ibrahim, who, let's be honest, would probably get yellow cards from their teachers every day if Mama didn't help them!"

She paused dramatically before delivering the pièce de résistance: "**Great Grandpa**, ***can these robots also tell us bedtime stories and sing cradle songs at night? Because if they can, it sounds like a dream come true! But... uh-oh," Maryam*** *suddenly looked concerned.* ***"What will be the role of Mama and Grandma then? And do you think the robots won't get angry if we ask them a thousand questions or request help with homework?"***

Great Grandpa chuckled heartily, his laughter as warm and comforting as a woolen shawl on a winter night. "Ah, **Maryam**, my dear inquisitive genius," he began, adjusting his spectacles and leaning back in his chair. "You paint quite a futuristic picture, but let me sprinkle in a bit of my wisdom here."

He leaned forward conspiratorially, a twinkle in his eyes. "First of all, robots may do all these wonderful tasks, but they'll lack one very important thing: *heart.* You see, **Maryam**, a robot can make coffee, but it can't brew it with love the way Grandma does. It might arrange **Yousuf** and **Ibrahim's** school bags, but it won't add that little note of encouragement Mama sometimes slips in."

Maryam's eyes widened, and she nodded, already sensing where this was going.

"Now about your bedtime stories," **Great Grandpa** continued, stroking his chin thoughtfully, "a robot might be able to tell you a tale, but will it know the right moment to make a scary face or soften its voice for the emotional parts? And as for cradle songs, my dear, a robot might sing, but will it ever hum with the same warmth and comfort as your Mama or Grandma when you snuggle up next to them? I doubt it."

Maryam giggled. *"But **Great Grandpa**, they won't get annoyed like humans do when we ask too many questions, right?"*

Great Grandpa's laughter filled the room again. "True, they might not get annoyed, but here's the catch: they might not understand why you're asking so many questions in the first place. Robots follow instructions, **Maryam**, but they can't understand curiosity. That's a human gift. It's what makes us explore, learn, and grow. You wouldn't want to lose that, would you?"

Maryam tilted her head, considering his words. "So, **Great Grandpa**, ***are you saying robots are good helpers, but they can't replace humans?"***

"Exactly, my little philosopher," **Great Grandpa** said, beaming with pride. "Robots can make life easier, but it's the imperfections, the quirks, and the love of real people—like your Mama and Grandma—that make life beautiful. Imagine a world where everything is perfect and predictable. No spilled juice, no forgotten books, no Mama chasing after **Yousuf** and **Ibrahim** with their tiffins—where's the fun in that?"

Maryam burst into laughter, picturing the chaos of her mornings. "You're right, **Great Grandpa**. Life would be boring without them!"

"And one last thing, my dear," **Great Grandpa** added with a wink, "even if robots bring you your coffee or orange juice, they might never know your secret snack stash. So who will sneak you cookies when Grandma's not looking?"

The room erupted in laughter, with **Maryam** clapping her hands in delight. "**Great Grandpa**, you're the best storyteller ever!"

"And you, **Maryam**," **Great Grandpa** said, ruffling her hair, "are the best question-asker ever. Never stop asking questions, my little wonder. That's how you'll always stay ahead of the robots!"

Maryam's eyes sparkled with a newfound question, and she leaned closer to **Great Grandpa** with an air of mystery. "Oh dearest **Great Grandpa,**" ***she began, dragging out her words like she was about to unveil the secret of the universe, "I almost forgot to ask you something super important!"***

Great Grandpa, who had been peacefully sipping lukewarm water, raised an eyebrow and smiled. "Oh? And what might that be, my little Einstein?"

Maryam's voice dropped to a whisper as if the walls had ears. ***"What about... the baby aliens?"***

Great Grandpa froze mid-sip, his eyes widening comically. "Baby... aliens?!"

"Yes!" ***Maryam*** *nodded, her excitement bubbling over.* ***"If we meet them in the future on Mars, will robots be able to catch hold of them? And—oh, this is the best part—help us make friendships with them? Like, imagine sharing knowledge about each other's worlds! Don't you think it could lead to amazing innovations for space and the cosmos?"***

Before **Great Grandpa** could respond, **Maryam's** imagination was already running wild. ***"And... if the aliens aren't friendly—like, what if they start throwing cosmic tantrums—do you think robots will protect us? You know, stand between us and the aliens, like superheroes with laser shields or something?"***

By now, **Great Grandpa** was laughing so hard he had to put down his tea to avoid spilling it. He wiped his eyes and looked at **Maryam** with mock seriousness. "Well, my dear **Maryam**, you've just given me a galactic-sized question to ponder. Let's break it down, shall we?"

Maryam nodded eagerly, her hands clasped like she was waiting for the punchline of the greatest joke ever told.

"First," **Great Grandpa** began, gesturing dramatically, "let's talk about the baby aliens. If they're anything like Earth babies, I'm guessing they'll be a mix of adorable and absolute chaos. Picture this: a Martian baby crawling around with green antennae, trying to nibble on your robots because it thinks they're toys!"

Maryam burst into giggles. ***"Oh no, poor robots! What would they do?"***

"Ah," **Great Grandpa** said, stroking his beard with mock wisdom, "the robots might politely say, 'Please refrain from chewing on me, dear alien infant.' But I doubt the baby aliens would understand. You see, robots are logical, but baby aliens? Pure mischief, just like human babies! So, catching hold of them might be harder than you think."

Maryam leaned in. ***"And making friends with them? Could robots help with that?"***

"Now that's a tricky one," **Great Grandpa** said, wagging his finger. "Robots might be able to translate alien languages or exchange scientific data, but can they offer a warm smile or a hearty laugh? Friendship isn't just about knowledge, **Maryam**—it's about feelings, trust, and sometimes sharing a chocolate bar. Can you imagine a robot offering a chocolate bar to a baby alien? They'd probably hand over the wrapper and keep the chocolate!"

Maryam howled with laughter. ***"Robots don't understand the real treasures of life, do they?"***

"Exactly!" **Great Grandpa** grinned. "Now, as for protecting us from angry aliens... that's where robots might shine. Picture this: robots forming a laser-shield barrier while we humans negotiate peace treaties. But here's the thing, **Maryam**—if we're ever lucky enough to meet aliens, it'll be up to *us* to prove that Earthlings are worth befriending. Robots might assist, but kindness, curiosity, and compassion? That's all us humans!"

Maryam thought about this for a moment. *"So,* ***Great Grandpa, are you saying that robots can be helpful but not enough on their own?"***

"Exactly, my little star-gazer," **Great Grandpa** said, his eyes twinkling. "Robots might build bridges across galaxies, but it's up to humans to cross them with open hearts. And as for those baby aliens? Well, I suggest you pack some extra cookies and chocolates. They might come in handy when making friends."

Maryam laughed so hard she nearly fell off her chair. "Oh, **Great Grandpa**, you always know how to make learning fun!"

"And you," **Great Grandpa** said, patting her head, "always know how to ask the most cosmic questions. Who knows? One day, you might be the one teaching robots and aliens how to be best friends!"

The question-answer session was in full swing, the family room buzzing with infectious laughter and excitement. **Great Grandpa,** ever the wise and playful orchestrator, clapped his hands with a smile that crinkled the corners of his eyes. "Alright, my little philosophers," he announced with mock seriousness, "it's time for a short break. Let's refuel those brilliant minds with some snacks and a glass of milk for the young ones—while I indulge in my favorite Sencha green tea. A storyteller needs his magic potion, after all!"

The children cheered, delighted at the prospect of a snack, while Grandma swooped in to arrange their treats. Even in the short pause, the room remained lively, buzzing with energy as everyone savored the moment.

Soon enough, plates were cleared, glasses were emptied, and **Great Grandpa** was back in his storytelling chair, rejuvenated and ready. **Ibrahim**, who had been quietly plotting his turn like a master strategist, sat up straighter. His mischievous grin hinted that his questions would be nothing short of legendary.

Great Grandpa leaned forward, his eyes sparkling with anticipation. "Ah, **Ibrahim**," he said, "the master of ideas! What wonders do you have in store for me today?"

The room fell into an expectant hush, and all eyes turned to **Ibrahim**, whose imagination was about to take center stage.

After the snack break, the family room reached peak energy, with Ibrahim, the self-proclaimed "master of ideas," taking center stage. His expression was a mix of deep thought and playful mischief as he adjusted his seat and cleared his throat dramatically.

"**Great Grandpa**," **Ibrahim** began, leaning forward with the intensity of a detective unveiling a groundbreaking theory. His wide-eyed excitement lit up the room. ***"My Papa is a Software Engineer and a really good developer. I think he could design software to control robots that could perform all types of surgeries—brain, heart, even replacing organs like kidneys, livers, or maybe even brains! Imagine extending human lives so people could be happy and healthy forever!"***

He paused dramatically as if waiting for gasps of astonishment. The room was hooked, but **Ibrahim** wasn't done. "*And you know what else,* ***Great Grandpa****?* ***If he programs a robot properly and updates it with all the AI stuff—it could even help him with his work! It could do all the software programming and development for him. Then, finally, he'd have more time to spend with me!"***

Ibrahim crossed his arms, his face glowing with triumph at the genius of his proposal.

Great Grandpa chuckled, his eyes twinkling as he leaned back in his chair, stroking his beard like a sage about to dispense timeless wisdom. "Ah, **Ibrahim**, so you think your Papa could revolutionize medicine *and* create a robot that would free him up to kick a football with you on weekends? That's quite the wish list!"

"Exactly!" **Ibrahim** said, bouncing on his toes, his enthusiasm bubbling over. *"He's always glued to his laptop, and he's too busy to play or take me on trips during holidays. If robots could handle everything, maybe we could finally have some fun!"*

The room erupted in laughter, the kind that shakes walls and makes cheeks ache. **Great Grandpa** raised his hand to calm the crowd, though his grin was impossible to hide.

"Ah, **Ibrahim**, my clever boy," he said, his voice brimming with amusement, "you've hit on an idea so brilliant, it might give your Papa's computer a headache. Imagine it: robots performing surgeries with no shaky hands, no delays, and no debates over hospital bills—just quick, painless procedures. Why, they might even have bedside manners if your Papa programs them right! But..."

Great Grandpa leaned in, lowering his voice conspiratorially, drawing everyone closer. "...let me tell you a secret about your Papa's job. It's not just about typing away at a keyboard. It's about thinking, imagining, and problem-solving—things robots can only dream of doing if they ever learn to dream! And let's face it, do you want a robot as your Papa? Would it tell you bedtime stories? Would it laugh at your silly jokes or share your love for ice cream? I think not!"

Ibrahim's face scrunched into a thoughtful expression as he considered this.

"But **Great Grandpa**," he persisted, ***"if the robot can work with Papa and do all the boring parts, he could still play football with me, right?"***

Great Grandpa laughed, his hearty chuckle echoing through the room. "Oh, you're sharp, my boy—sharp as a tack! Maybe one day your Papa *will* design a robot to help him with his work. But until then, let's try this: why don't you go sit next to him while he works? Watch him code, learn a trick or two, and maybe even help him out. Who knows? You might just inspire him to take a break and kick that football with you sooner than you think!"

The room burst into applause as **Ibrahim** grinned from ear to ear, already plotting his next move to win his Papa's time—and maybe even his help designing that robot!

Ibrahim's eyes widened. "But what?"

"But," **Great Grandpa** continued with a twinkle in his eye, "you forgot something important—surgeons don't just heal with their hands. They heal with their hearts. A robot might replace a kidney, but it can't hold your hand and say, 'Don't worry, you'll be fine.' So, while robots might assist, your Papa's next big project should also include *empathy software*. Otherwise, patients will be leaving the hospital cured but lonely!"

The room roared with laughter, and **Ibrahim** nodded thoughtfully. "Okay, **Great Grandpa**, I'll suggest that to Papa. But I have another question—this one's BIG."

"Ah, the big guns!" **Great Grandpa** said, pretending to brace himself. "Fire away, Commander **Ibrahim**."

"**Great Grandpa**," **Ibrahim** began, his tone turning serious, ***"can robots and artificial intelligence run parliaments or organize international assemblies like the United Nations? Because right now, most parliaments are full of corrupt politicians creating chaos. They lie, fight, and make decisions that harm the majority of innocent people. They misuse taxpayers' money and dominate weaker nations. Couldn't intelligent robots take over and run things honestly—no bias, no corruption, no bad behavior?"***

Great Grandpa let out a hearty laugh. "Oh, **Ibrahim**, you've outdone yourself this time! Imagine a parliament full of robots—no shouting, no table thumping, no food fights, no chair throwing! They'd analyze data, make unbiased decisions, and pass laws faster than your Mama packs your school tiffin."

"Exactly!" **Ibrahim** said, beaming. ***"They wouldn't care about religion, gender, or color. They'd ensure human rights for everyone. Even***

global summits like the G-20 wouldn't waste billions on fancy meals and travel. Robots could handle everything remotely, with no need for extravagant expenses!"

Great Grandpa clapped his hands. "And imagine the speeches—just a robot saying, 'Agenda complete. Thank you. Meeting adjourned.' Short, sweet, and no political drama! But here's the catch, my boy."

"What catch?" **Ibrahim** asked, intrigued.

"Robots might solve the problem of dishonesty," **Great Grandpa** said, "but they can't solve the problem of humanity. Decisions about people's lives need a human touch—compassion, understanding, and sometimes, compromise. Robots might run things logically, but what happens when a situation calls for forgiveness, or when nations need to mend relationships built on trust? That's where humans must step up."

The family nodded thoughtfully, but **Ibrahim** wasn't done yet. *"But* ***Great Grandpa****, **wouldn't it be amazing if robots did take over? Imagine—a world without corruption, with every decision made for the greater good. No more dishonest leaders, no more dominance by mighty nations. Just fairness and justice for all!"***

Great Grandpa smiled warmly. "Ah, Ibrahim, you dream of a world where robots bring a sigh of relief to humanity. But let me tell you a secret—robots might be tools for change, but the real power lies in teaching humans to act like the robots you're imagining: honest, unbiased, and fair. So, instead of waiting for robots to save us, maybe we should start building that world ourselves."

Ibrahim grinned. "Wow, **Great Grandpa**, ***you make it sound like we need upgrading!"***

The room filled with laughter, and **Great Grandpa** leaned in, his eyes twinkling. "Well, if your Papa writes that empathy software, maybe he can design one for us humans too—Version 2.0: Kinder, Wiser, and Less Prone to Fighting in Parliaments!"

Everyone burst into laughter, and the session continued with an air of wonder and joy, fueled by Ibrahim's boundless curiosity and Great Grandpa's wisdom wrapped in humor.

Ibrahim was not fully satisfied with the response of his **Great-Grandpa**, he leaned forward, his expression perplexed and his young mind buzzing with questions. "**Great Grandpa**,*"he began, his voice tinged with frustration. I'm not comfortable with how things are moving in the world today. Everything feels off balance!"*

Great Grandpa adjusted his glasses, smiling at **Ibrahim's** intensity. "Tell me what's on your mind, dear boy. Let's dissect it together!"

Ibrahim took a deep breath, and the words came tumbling out like a waterfall:
"Everybody is so busy and occupied, running like headless chickens—at markets, airports, railways, bus stations—but somehow, nobody seems to reach their destinations on time.

People are exercising, doing yoga, and running in the mornings and evenings, but not a single one of them looks truly healthy. Moral centers are popping up everywhere—in cities, towns, and even villages—but morality itself seems to be missing.

Everyone is chasing careers with all their might, but no one is satisfied once they get there. They're working around the clock to achieve their milestones, but we're all missing some deeper goals.

It's like we're all busy for nothing, Great Grandpa! Can't we create something... a nicely well-planned robot or AI system... that can take care of us and fix these issues? Humanity seems tense and disturbed. Be honest with me, Great Grandpa—don't dodge my question!"

Great Grandpa leaned back in his chair, his eyes twinkling with wisdom and a dash of humor. "Ah, **Ibrahim**, you remind me of myself at your age—bursting with questions and not afraid to challenge the world!"

He chuckled before continuing. "Let me try to answer you honestly, my dear boy. The world today does indeed feel like a race, but do you know the problem? It's not the race itself—it's that we've forgotten the finish line. Everyone's running, but no one knows where they're running to! We're like marathoners with no map, just circling the track endlessly."

Ibrahim nodded eagerly. ***"Exactly, Great Grandpa! So, what's the solution? Is it robotics?"***

Great Grandpa laughed heartily, the kind that made the room feel lighter. "Robotics, eh? Oh, I see—you want to build a 'Super Nanny Bot' to take care of humanity! Let me tell you a little secret, **Ibrahim**. A robot can fetch you tea, remind you to exercise, and even recite moral quotes—but can it laugh with you when you spill the tea? Can it share a story that stirs your soul? Can it understand the joy of a sunrise or the sorrow of a tear? Robots are tools, my boy—not teachers, not companions, and not problem-solvers for the human heart."

Ibrahim looked thoughtful. ***"So... are you saying we're the problem? That we need to fix ourselves instead of creating robots to do it for us?"***

Great Grandpa's face softened. "That's exactly what I'm saying. Humanity's tension isn't from being busy—it's from being disconnected. From ourselves, from each other, and our Creator. We don't need robots to fix us, **Ibrahim**. We need to slow down, breathe, and remember what truly matters—kindness, laughter, family, faith. And maybe, just maybe, a game of chess with your **Great Grandpa**!"

Ibrahim laughed, the weight of his earlier frustration lifting. ***"So, you're saying we already have what we need to fix things?"***

"Precisely, my boy," said **Great Grandpa**, a mischievous twinkle in his eye. "Now, how about we build that robot—not to solve humanity's problems, but to clean up my study? It's getting harder for me to reach the corners!"

They all burst out laughing, the tension in the air replaced by joy. And **Ibrahim** couldn't help but think that **Great Grandpa**'s answers had soothed his mind like a gentle balm, leaving him with more to ponder—and a heart full of hope.

After a long wait and plenty of chuckles at previous exchanges, it was finally **Yousuf's** turn. With a glint of excitement in his eyes, he stood up dramatically and declared, "**Great Grandpa**, ***I've got a whole bag of questions about the future of robots! My mind is constantly buzzing, but nobody has been able to answer me properly—certainly not in a way that lets me sleep peacefully at night."***

Great Grandpa leaned back in his armchair, adjusting his glasses. "Ah, **Yousuf**, my dearest boy! Go ahead. Ask me your questions. I'll do my best to answer them with all the wisdom I've gathered over the years—and I promise you this: by the end of tonight, you'll sleep peacefully. But make sure to set an alarm and wake up in time to catch your school bus tomorrow morning!"

The family erupted in laughter, and **Yousu**f, grinning from ear to ear, began his volley of questions.

Yousuf: ***"How might robots be used to manage natural disasters like earthquakes, floods, or forest fires like the ones in LA- US, hurricanes, or man-made crises like nuclear accidents or carbon emissions driving up global temperatures? What are the benefits and limitations?"***

Great Grandpa: "Ah, **Yousu**f, that's a brilliant question! Let me paint you a picture. Imagine a fleet of robots with specialized abilities: drones flying into burning forests, spraying water and mapping out fire patterns; ground robots navigating rubble in earthquake zones to locate survivors; or underwater robots repairing flood-damaged infrastructure. Sounds incredible, doesn't it?"

Yousuf nodded eagerly.

"But," **Great Grandpa** continued, raising a finger, "here's the catch—robots can't predict a forest fire before it starts or stop a tsunami from forming. They're excellent assistants but terrible magicians. And don't forget, they need humans to program them, maintain them, and make the ethical decisions they're incapable of. So while robots can save lives and mitigate disasters, the real responsibility still lies with us—to act wisely, plan, and prevent these crises where we can. Remember, **Yousuf**, even the smartest robot can't replace common sense and care for our planet."

Yousuf: ***"What about robots for surveillance and intelligence gathering in other countries? How do we balance security needs with privacy concerns?"***

Great Grandpa: "Ah, now you're diving into murky waters, young man. Surveillance robots can certainly help catch the bad guys—they can fly high, zoom in with cameras, and even sniff out explosives. But imagine this: a nosy little drone hovering outside your bedroom window while you're doing homework. How would you feel about that?"

Yousuf frowned. "I wouldn't like it one bit!"

"Exactly," said **Great Grandpa**. "That's the dilemma. On one hand, robots can make the world safer by gathering intelligence and preventing crimes. On the other hand, they can be used to spy on ordinary people, invading privacy and creating distrust. The solution? Balance. We need strict rules and wise leaders to ensure robots are used for security—not snooping into people's lives. And if a robot does cross the line, well, I suggest we program them to apologize with a bouquet!"

The family burst into laughter again.

Yousuf: ***"Looking ahead, what new roles do you think robots will play in our daily lives, and how can we ensure they're developed and used responsibly?"***

Great Grandpa: "Oh, the future is as bright as your smile, **Yousuf**! Robots might do everything from cooking your meals and cleaning your room—

yes, even that disaster zone you call a desk—to being your study buddies, reminding you about school projects. They could assist the elderly, plant crops, and maybe even play cricket with you in the backyard!"

Yousuf's eyes widened with excitement. "That sounds amazing!"

"But," **Great Grandpa** added, leaning in, "there's a big *if*. These robots must be developed responsibly. That means no cutting corners, no shortcuts in testing, and no putting profits above safety. And we must always ask ourselves: 'Is this helping humanity, or harming it?' The answer to that question will guide us to use robots wisely."

Great-grandpa looked at **Yousuf** fondly. "You see, my boy, robots are like tools—they're as good or bad as the people who wield them. If we fill the world with robots but forget to fill our hearts with kindness, compassion, and wisdom, then even the smartest robots won't save us. But if we use them to amplify our humanity, well, that's a future worth dreaming of."

Yousuf clapped his hands, a huge smile spreading across his face. "Thank you, **Great Grandpa!** Now I think I *will* sleep peacefully tonight."

"And don't forget the school bus, **Yousuf**!" **Great Grandpa** said with a wink, as the family room filled with laughter once more.

The children, still buzzing with curiosity, weren't entirely satisfied with the earlier answers. Their wide-eyed wonder demanded more convincing responses from **Great Grandpa**. So, with unyielding determination, they fired off a barrage of questions, diving deeper into the great Robot Debate, the Cure Conundrum, the dreams of domestic robot helpers, and the ever-looming Cyber Threat Crisis. They were eager for clarity, and a touch of **Great Grandpa**'s wisdom to quench their growing curiosity.

The Great Robot Debate

Yousuf: Great Grandpa, "do you think we can build friendly robots one day that remind us to eat good, healthy food—and stop us when we try to eat junk that's bad for our bodies"?

Great Grandpa: Ah, my curious little scientist! What a brilliant idea you've just sparked! Yes, indeed—we *can* make such robots. In fact, people are already working on machines and apps that help guide our eating habits. But imagine a kind, talking robot at your dining table, gently saying, "**Yousuf**, try some fruits instead of that chocolate!" Or maybe it could even sing a little song when you choose healthy food—just like a cheerleader for your tummy!

You see, our body is like a wonderful machine too. And just like a car needs clean fuel, our body needs good food to stay strong, smart, and happy. So if we make robots to help us choose wisely, they would become our best health buddies!

And who knows… maybe *you* will be the one to invent such a robot for children all over the world! Wouldn't that be something?

Great-Grandchild: ***"Great Grandpa, will we even need doctors in the future? Imagine a robotic oncologist eliminating cancer, a robotic cardiothoracic surgeon seamlessly transplanting hearts, or even robotic neurosurgeons performing miracles—like replacing brains if science allows! Will diseases be treated with flawless precision?"***

Great Grandpa: *(laughing)* "Oh, my curious little scientist! While I'd love to see robots solving these complex puzzles, don't expect them to be superheroes just yet. Robots may perform surgeries with remarkable accuracy, but remember, it's the human heart—not just the mechanical hands—that often heals the patient. Bedside manners don't come pre-programmed! Besides, would you want a robot to diagnose your bellyache without a single empathetic pat on your head? Robots can assist, but I doubt they'll replace the magic of human doctors anytime soon. And about replacing brains—mine has worked overtime for decades, but it's still not available in the spare parts catalog!"

The Cure Conundrum

Great-Grandchild: ***"Great Grandpa, do you think AI could create vaccines for cancer, like we did for COVID-19 and polio? Cancer is still the second leading cause of death worldwide. Can we unlock the ultimate cure, or will it remain one of humanity's greatest challenges?"***

Great Grandpa: "That's a wonderful dream, my dear. AI is already helping scientists understand cancer better—finding patterns in data that humans could miss. Could it lead to a vaccine? Maybe! But cancer is like a clever villain—it keeps changing its disguise. While AI can give us the tools, it's up to human ingenuity and determination to use them wisely. Solving cancer might not be a single 'Eureka!' moment. It's a marathon, not a sprint. And remember, hope itself is a powerful medicine—it keeps humanity innovating, imagining, and striving for the seemingly impossible."

Domestic Dreamers

Great-Grandchild: ***"Great Grandpa, imagine domestic robots serving morning tea to retirees, reminding them to take their medications, and even keeping the house clean. No more waiting for servants stuck in traffic! But will robots truly make life easier for everyone?"***

Great Grandpa: "Ah, a robot to bring me my tea—I'd sign up for that right away! But life might get a bit dull without some good old human chaos. Robots may excel at routine tasks, but can they match the joy of sharing a laugh with the milkman or the gossip with your neighbor? Besides, robots will need energy, maintenance, and constant upgrades—sounds a bit like your great-grandma managing me! Life might become easier in some ways, but true happiness comes from connections, not just convenience. Robots can't tuck you into bed with a bedtime story, can they?"

The Cyber Threat Crisis

Great-Grandchild: ***"Great Grandpa, we've heard AI could also be dangerous. Imagine AI-powered hackers stealing bank information or withdrawing money by intercepting OTPs. How can we stay safe from these kinds of crimes?"***

Great Grandpa: "Ah, the dark side of the AI moon! Cybercrime is a real threat, my child, but every lock has a key—every problem has a solution. To stay safe, we need to stay smart. Use strong passwords—longer than the queue at the barber shop on Eid! Avoid sharing sensitive information over calls or messages. And remember, just like you'd think twice before opening the door to a stranger, think twice before clicking that shady link promising a free treasure chest! Most importantly, technology should serve us, not scare us. If we combine caution with curiosity, we'll always stay a step ahead of those digital troublemakers."

Great-grandpa took a deep breath, his eyes reflecting both concern and wisdom. "**Ibrahim**, cybercrimes and financial frauds have evolved into a never-ending battle between security measures and criminal ingenuity. No matter how many precautions we take, technology itself is a double-edged sword—it empowers us, but also equips criminals with new tools.

Your friend's father is a victim of what we call 'financial cybercrime,' which includes identity theft, phishing scams, and unauthorized transactions. Banks and law enforcement agencies have established protocols, but cybercriminals often stay one step ahead by exploiting loopholes in digital security systems. Once the money is transferred to offshore accounts or converted into untraceable assets like cryptocurrency, retrieval becomes nearly impossible.

Now, you ask whether there is an end to this. Theoretically, no—because as long as digital technology evolves, so will cyber threats. However, we can minimize the risks through constant technological advancements in cybersecurity, AI-driven fraud detection, and global cooperation in cyber law enforcement. In the future, biometric authentication, blockchain-based banking, and real-time monitoring by AI may reduce such frauds, but criminals will keep finding new ways to bypass them.

The key lies in continuous awareness and proactive defense—stronger authentication measures, smarter regulatory frameworks, and personal vigilance. The fight is not about 'eliminating' crime but staying ahead in the race against it."

He sighed, then added, "The world is changing fast, my dear **Ibrahim**. The best we can do is educate ourselves, adapt, and remain cautious."

Great-Grandpa chuckled softly, leaning forward with a knowing look. "Ah, **Ibrahim**, you have put it beautifully! Yes, AI is like a grand palace with two doors—one that welcomes innovation and progress, and the other, a secret passage where cybercriminals sneak in, their pockets lined with stolen wealth.

You see, every great invention in history has been a double-edged sword. The printing press spread knowledge but also propaganda. Electricity powered homes but also brought electrocution risks. The internet connected the world but also opened pathways for cybercrime. AI is no different—it holds the power to protect, yet it also empowers those with malicious intent.

Now, does that mean we are helpless? Not at all! Just as kings of old-built fortresses with higher walls and smarter guards, today's AI developers are building stronger defenses—advanced encryption, real-time fraud detection, and self-learning security systems that predict and block cyberattacks before they happen. However, criminals, too, are using AI, creating sophisticated scams that mimic human behavior so well that even banks and police struggle to detect them.

So, the battle is not about shutting the backdoor completely—it's about constantly upgrading the lock, making it harder for criminals to find a way in. And most importantly, it's about people—people like you and me—staying aware, questioning unusual activities, and never handing over the 'keys' of our digital world so easily.

AI is not the villain, my dear **Ibrahim**. It's a powerful tool in the hands of both the righteous and the rogue. Who wins? That depends on how wisely we use it."

Great-Grandpa leaned forward, his eyes twinkling with curiosity. "Ah, **Ibrahim**, you've touched on a subject that is making waves across the world! Yes, I've heard about DeepSeek AI, the latest marvel from Chinese scientists. It's said to be built with highly advanced algorithms and a powerful multi-chip architecture, giving it superior computational abilities. Some reports claim it processes data more efficiently than existing AI models like Meta AI, Claude 3.5, and Google Gemini.

Now, why has this caused a stir in the U.S. stock market? Well, AI is not just about technology—it's about power, competition, and economic influence. You see, the AI industry is like a high-stakes chess game between global superpowers. The U.S. has dominated AI development for years, but if China's DeepSeek AI truly surpasses existing models, it could shift the balance of technological and economic leadership.

Investors reacted quickly because AI advancements directly impact industries, automation, and even military capabilities. If China gains an upper hand in AI, it could influence everything from global finance to cybersecurity, making U.S. companies and policymakers uneasy. That uncertainty led to turbulence in the stock markets, as investors recalibrated their expectations.

But let me tell you something, my dear boy—this is just another chapter in the ongoing AI race. Whenever one nation leaps forward, others respond with even greater innovations. So while DeepSeek AI is making headlines today, rest assured that teams at OpenAI, Google, and other tech giants are already working on even more advanced models. The AI race never truly stops—it only accelerates."

Great-grandpa chuckled, tapping Ibrahim's shoulder. "The real question isn't about which AI is the most powerful—it's about how humanity chooses to use it. Will AI be a tool for progress or a force for control and manipulation? That, Ibrahim, is what we must keep our eyes on."

By this point, even **Great-Grandpa**, with all his wisdom and endurance, felt the weight of the deep discussions. Ibrahim's relentless curiosity had sparked an intense debate, and everyone had been drawn into the whirlwind of knowledge, excitement, and speculation. But now, minds were full, voices were hoarse, and it was clear—this session had run its course.

With a unanimous nod, they agreed to pause the discussion, letting the thrill of unanswered questions linger until next weekend. Tomorrow was Sunday, a day reserved for something entirely different—a break from AI, cybercrimes, and global power struggles. The family had long set their sights on a full-day adventure to the stunning Half Moon Beach along the Pacific Ocean. The thought of salty sea breezes, golden sand between their toes, and the rhythmic crashing of waves promised a perfect escape from the complexities of technology.

But that wasn't all. After basking in the coastal serenity, the journey would continue to the famous Mystery Spot in San Francisco—a place where gravity seemed to play tricks, and perception defied logic. **Great-grandpa** chuckled at the thought. "From AI mysteries to real-life optical illusions—it seems like we are destined to explore the unknown, one way or another!"

With laughter filling the air, the family wrapped up their evening, already looking forward to a day of sun, sand, and spine-tingling mystery. The intellectual battles would resume soon enough—but for now, adventure called!

If all went according to plan, the next session might resume the following Saturday when everyone agreed to reconvene. This meeting had been nothing short of a rollercoaster—highly entertaining, packed with fascinating insights, and bursting with unexpected revelations. It even turned into a challenging IQ test for **Great Grandpa**, who had risen to the occasion like a true champion.

As the session drew to a close, the three grandchildren threw their arms around **Great-Grandpa** in a warm, heartfelt group hug. With laughter echoing in the air and promises to reconvene soon, the gathering was adjourned on a high note, leaving everyone eagerly anticipating their next lively exchange.

Session Five

Yesterday's Vision, Tomorrow's Reality

Past Meets Future

Great Grandpa and the Kids: Exploring AI, Robots, Ethics, and the Future of Work and War

It felt like an eternity for the **great-grandpa** as the weekdays slipped by, with the children buried in their busy routines, juggling classes and homework. But at last, Friday evening arrived—a moment eagerly awaited by all. The **great-grandpa** and his **great-grandchildren** beamed with joy as they reunited for another lively session of mighty conversations, brimming with endless fun and hearty laughter.

The morning air was crisp, filled with the promise of an exciting day ahead. The children, looking fresh and full of energy, had slept soundly the night before—no haunting dreams of unfinished homework to trouble their young minds. Even **Great-Grandpa**, with his usual wisdom and warmth, looked especially lively, rejuvenated by a night of deep, peaceful sleep.

Overnight, the family room had taken on a whole new charm. Grandma, with her artistic touch, had adorned the walls with her latest handmade paintings—vivid landscapes, serene natural scenes, and a few abstract masterpieces that sparked curiosity and imagination. The once-familiar space now felt refreshingly new, a perfect setting for another lively family gathering. **Great-grandpa**, appreciating the transformation, took out his phone to capture a video, preserving the moment as a cherished memory for years to come.

Soon, the children, dressed in bright, colorful outfits and with their hair neatly combed, came bouncing down the stairs. Their laughter filled the room as they greeted each other in perfect harmony, "**Good morning, Great-Grandpa!"**

Great-grandpa beamed, his eyes twinkling with joy. "A very good morning, my charming little stars!" he replied, his voice rich with affection. The children giggled and settled beside his armchair, their eager faces reflecting the excitement of being together again after a whole week.

There was something magical about these moments—an unspoken bond, a silent understanding that this was more than just a conversation; it was a tradition, a treasure trove of wisdom, laughter, and love.

Great-grandpa looked around at his beloved **great grandchildren**, nodding in approval. "So, my young explorers," he said, his tone playful yet thoughtful, "I hope you're all doing well. Are we ready for another session of discovery and wonder?"

The children shot each other thrilled glances, their eyes sparkling with curiosity and excitement. A brand-new discussion was about to begin—one that would finally clear up some lingering mysteries that had been buzzing in their minds. And they knew one thing for sure—whenever **Great-Grandpa** spoke, it wasn't just a conversation; it was a journey into a world of wisdom, wonder, and adventure!

Maryam Takes the Lead Once Again!

As usual, **Maryam**, with her curious mind and fearless questioning, started the conversation.

Maryam: Great Grandpa, ***"technology is changing everything around us! Artificial intelligence (AI) is improving data analysis, cybersecurity, and even how we experience the internet. Robots are taking over manufacturing, and self-driving cars will soon be everywhere! Not to mention space technology—robots and AI are helping us explore the universe. How do you feel about all these changes?"***

Great-Grandpa (grinning): Ah, **Maryam**! You're back with another round of tricky questions. Let's see if my old brain can keep up. But first, let me grab my glasses... Oh, wait—they're already on my nose! *Hah!* I think I need AI just to remind me where I keep my stuff!

1. Artificial Intelligence & Communication

Maryam: AI is getting so smart! It can analyze huge amounts of data, protect our online security, and even recommend what we should watch or buy. Isn't that amazing?

Great-Grandpa: Amazing? Sure! But also a little creepy! Have you ever searched for a pair of shoes online, and then suddenly, every website starts showing you shoe ads? It's like AI is spying on you—"Oh, you like red sneakers? Here, have 500 more ads!"

AI is brilliant at finding patterns, but it's not thinking. If I tell AI, "Find me a joke," it might show me something funny. But if I say, "Tell me a joke about how I keep losing my glasses," AI would probably get confused.

AI is like a parrot—it can repeat things very well, but it doesn't *truly* understand. That's why, no matter how smart AI gets, humans will always have the upper hand. After all, AI can write poetry, but can it laugh at its bad jokes? I don't think so!

2. Robotics in Manufacturing:

Maryam: Robots are making cars, assembling phones, and even cooking food in some places! Do you think they'll take all the jobs one day?

Great-Grandpa: Let's see... Can robots clean the floor? Yes. Can they make perfect pancakes? Yes. Can they argue with your mom about what to cook for dinner? No! *Hah!*

Robots are great at repetitive, boring tasks, but they can't replace jobs that need emotions, creativity, or human interaction. I mean, would you want a robot teacher at school? Imagine asking, "Can you explain that again?" and the robot says, "Error 404: Explanation Not Found!"

Besides, who will *fix* the robots when they break down? Humans! So, don't worry—jobs will change, but we won't run out of work. After all, someone still needs to teach these robots some manners!

3. Self-Driving Cars & Smart Transport:

Maryam: Self-driving cars are coming soon! No more traffic jams, no more accidents—just smooth, intelligent transport. Isn't that incredible?

Great-Grandpa: Oh, **Maryam**, you haven't seen how I drive! Even a self-driving car would get confused—"Do I follow traffic rules or Great-Grandpa's shortcuts?"

Self-driving cars are a great idea, but they have one big problem: they follow *logic*, while humans… Well, we don't always do that! If a ball rolls onto the road, a human knows a child might be running after it. AI? It just sees a ball and thinks, "No need to stop."

And imagine this: Your car takes a wrong turn, and you shout, "Hey, stop!" But instead of stopping, it politely replies, "Recalculating route." By the time it figures it out, you're in another city!

So, until self-driving cars can understand *real* human behavior—like how people honk even when they're wrong—I think I'll stick to my old bicycle.

4. Space Exploration & AI

Maryam: AI is helping scientists discover new planets, analyze space data, and even run Mars rovers. Do you think humans will live on Mars one day?

Great-Grandpa: Live on Mars? Hmm, let me think. Mars has:

1. No Oxygen
2. No water
3. Freezing temperatures
4. Dust storms that last for months

Sounds like a great vacation spot, doesn't it? *Hah!*

Sure, AI is helping us explore space, but Mars isn't exactly paradise. You'd need a space suit *just* to step outside. And don't even get me started on the food—freeze-dried potatoes every day? No, thank you!

We might *visit* Mars, but living there? Not unless someone finds a way to deliver hot, fresh biryani!

Final Thought:

Maryam: So, do you think AI and robots are good or bad?

Great-Grandpa: Ah, my dear, technology is like fire. Fire can cook your food or burn your house down—it all depends on how we use it.

AI can help doctors detect diseases early, but it can also spread fake news. Self-driving cars can make travel safer, but they can also malfunction. Robots can help humans, but they can't replace the warmth of a real hug.

So, the secret is balance! Use AI wisely, but don't *depend* on it for everything. After all, you wouldn't want AI deciding what you should wear every day. Imagine wearing polka-dotted pajamas to a wedding because the algorithm thought it was "trendy"!

And speaking of AI… can someone invent a robot that finds lost glasses? Because I just lost mine *again!*

Maryam (laughing): ***Oh, Great Grandpa! You don't need AI, you just need a pocket to keep your glasses in!***

Great Grandpa: Ah-ha! But a pocket doesn't beep and tell me, "Hey, your glasses are here!" Now *that* would be useful AI!

Ibrahim Joins the Live Discussion!

After **Maryam** wrapped up her round of questions, **Ibrahim**, who had been quietly listening, leaned forward with a determined look.

Ibrahim: Great Grandpa, ***I have a big question! Climate change is becoming a huge problem, and I keep hearing that AI is helping to solve it. People say AI can predict climate patterns, optimize resource usage, and develop sustainable solutions to protect the environment. "Can you explain how all of this works and clarify my doubts?"***

Great-Grandpa (chuckling): Ah, **Ibrahim**! You've brought a real *earth-shaking* question today—literally! Climate change is no joke. The summers are getting hotter, winters are getting unpredictable, and even my knees seem to detect the changing weather better than the forecast!

But you're right—AI is playing a big role in fighting climate change. "Let me explain this in a way that feels less like a dull science lecture and more like an exciting journey into how AI is shaping our everyday lives."

1. Predicting Climate Patterns

Ibrahim: ***How does AI predict climate patterns? Can it tell us the future of the weather?***

Great-Grandpa: Ah, if only AI could predict the weather perfectly, I'd know whether to carry an umbrella or not!

But here's how it works—AI analyzes massive amounts of data from satellites, ocean sensors, and weather stations. It looks at past climate patterns, spots trends, and then predicts what might happen next. It's like how your mom knows when you're about to sneak into the kitchen for an extra piece of cake—she's seen the pattern too many times!

For example, AI can detect rising ocean temperatures and predict hurricanes before they form. It can warn farmers about droughts or floods so they can plan. And it can help governments prepare for extreme weather so people don't end up stranded in floods or caught in heatwaves.

But does AI get it right *all* the time? Nope! Even the smartest models can't control nature. It's like when I set an alarm for 6 AM, but my body decides it prefers 9 AM instead. *Hah!*

2. Optimizing Resource Usage

Ibrahim: ***People say AI helps save energy and resources. How does it do that?***

Great-Grandpa: Ah, now this is where AI shines!

Imagine this—you leave the lights, fan, and TV on even when you leave the room (I'm looking at *you*, Ibrahim!). Now imagine if your house was *smart* enough to notice this and turn them off automatically. AI does something similar but on a much *bigger* scale!

For example:

✅ AI-powered smart grids help reduce electricity waste by predicting how much energy a city needs at different times.

✅ Factories use AI to cut down water and power waste by making machines run more efficiently.

✅ AI even helps farmers! It analyzes soil data and tells farmers the *exact* amount of water and fertilizer needed, reducing waste and pollution.

It's like having a super-intelligent grandma who tells you, "Stop wasting food! Take only what you need." Except AI won't pinch your ears if you don't listen!

3. Developing Sustainable Solutions

Ibrahim: *AI is also being used to create eco-friendly solutions. What kind of things has it invented?*

Great-Grandpa: Ah, now *this* is where AI is doing some amazing work!

- AI and Renewable Energy: AI helps wind turbines and solar panels work smarter by predicting the best times to generate power. It also manages battery storage so we can use solar energy at night and wind energy on calm days.
- AI and Pollution Control: AI-powered robots are cleaning up oceans by identifying and removing plastic waste. AI also helps monitor air pollution levels and suggests ways to reduce emissions from factories and cars.
- AI and Recycling: Some AI machines can now separate recyclable waste from trash more accurately than humans. Imagine a robot looking at a pile of garbage and saying, "This bottle can be recycled, but this chip packet cannot!"—all without holding its nose!

AI is like an environmental superhero—it doesn't wear a cape, but it's trying to save the planet one smart decision at a time!

4. Can AI Save the Planet?

Ibrahim: *So, **Great-Grandpa, does this mean AI will stop climate change completely?***

Great-Grandpa (laughing)**:** Ah, my dear **Ibrahim**, if AI alone could save the planet, we'd all be sitting back and eating ice cream by now!

AI is a tool, not a magic wand. It can help predict problems, find better ways to use resources, and even suggest solutions—but it can't change human behavior.

If people keep polluting the environment, cutting down forests, and wasting resources, no amount of AI can fix that! AI can tell us how to live more sustainably, but it's up to *us* to listen and take action.

It's like this—if you keep leaving your socks all over the house, your mom might use AI to set reminders for you. But unless *you* decide to clean up, the mess will still be there!

So, AI can guide us, but saving the planet is still *our* responsibility. We need to be smarter about how we live, just like AI is making technology smarter.

Final Thought:

Ibrahim: Wow, **great grandpa**! ***So AI is like a super-smart assistant, but we still have to do our part?***

Great Grandpa: Exactly, my boy! AI is like having a GPS—it can tell you the best route, but *you* still have to drive the car.

Now, speaking of saving resources... Do you think AI can help me find my missing socks? I swear, every time I put two in the wash, only one comes back! Maybe my washing machine has a secret black hole!

Ibrahim (laughing)**: Great Grandpa**, ***I think you need AI just to keep track of all the things you misplace!***

Great-Grandpa: That, my dear **Ibrahim**, is the *best* use of AI I've heard so far!

Ibrahim: Great Grandpa, ***I have a big question that's been bothering me! Everyone keeps talking about how climate change is one of the biggest threats to our planet. You've explained how AI is being used to fight it—how it can predict extreme weather, optimize energy use, and even help cut down pollution. But if AI is so advanced, why is the climate crisis still worsening?***

Shouldn't things be improving by now? Or is AI just a small piece of the puzzle? What about world leaders, governments, and global organizations—aren't they the ones with real power to make a difference? Are they taking the right steps, or are they failing us?

I want to understand, Great-Grandpa—how must AI and leadership work together to truly save our planet? And if they don't act fast enough, what will happen to our future?

Great-Grandpa's Response:

Ah, my dear **great-grandson**, you've asked a very important question! Climate change is indeed a serious threat, and while AI is playing a role in combating it, the real responsibility lies with world leaders, heads of states, and global organizations. They have the power to create policies, enforce laws, and drive action on a massive scale. Let me explain how they, along with AI, can work together to protect our planet:

- Policy & Regulations: Governments must enforce strict environmental laws to control carbon emissions, reduce deforestation, and promote clean energy. AI helps by monitoring industrial emissions, tracking deforestation via satellite images, and predicting the impact of policies.
- Renewable Energy Management: Leaders must invest in solar, wind, and hydro energy. AI-powered smart grids optimize electricity usage, reducing waste and making renewable energy more efficient.
- Disaster Prediction & Preparedness: AI analyzes climate data to predict natural disasters like hurricanes, wildfires, and floods. Governments must act on these warnings, building better infrastructure and evacuating people when needed.
- Sustainable Agriculture: AI helps farmers use water and fertilizers efficiently, reducing waste and pollution. But leaders must ensure farmers have access to AI-powered tools and education.
- Global Cooperation: Climate change is a global crisis, and no single country can solve it alone. World leaders must unite, agree on strict climate policies, and hold each other accountable. AI can provide real-time data on carbon footprints and climate progress to ensure transparency.
- Public Awareness & Action: Governments must educate people about climate change and encourage eco-friendly habits like reducing plastic use, conserving water, and using public transport. AI helps by analyzing data on human behavior and suggesting better policies for environmental protection.

So, my dear child, AI is a tool—a very powerful one—but the real change must come from the decisions and actions of our leaders. They must put the planet before profit, take responsibility, and act before it's too late!

Ibrahim: Oh yes! I realize that AI and world leaders must join hands—honestly and sincerely—to tackle climate change. If they do, it'll be a huge relief for the planet and future generations like us!

Great-Grandpa:

Great Grandpa: Haha, my dear Ibrahim, AI can predict storms, but it can't stop politicians from creating them! AI is smart, but without wise and honest leadership, it's like having a spaceship with no pilot. If world leaders truly work with AI—not just for speeches but for real action—maybe, just maybe, we won't need to build underwater cities in the future!

Finally Yousuf Joins the Live Discussion:

Yousuf had been quietly listening, his young mind absorbing every detail of the conversation, his heart wrestling with the weight of the world's tragedies. The silence in the room was thick with unspoken thoughts, but then, with a sudden, overwhelming sorrow, he let out a loud cry. His small hands trembled as he reached for his **great-grandfather**, his voice choked with emotion.

"**Great Grandpa!**" he sobbed, his chest heaving. ***"Why do the world's most powerful nations continue to wage wars? Why so much destruction? So much suffering? Genocides? Innocent men, women, and even little children—what could they have possibly done to deserve such pain? Why must they pay the price for decisions made in places they'll never even see?"***

His **great-grandfather**, an old man with decades of experience etched into the lines of his face, felt his own heart break at the sight of **Yousuf**'s anguish. He pulled the boy into his lap, wrapping his arms tightly around him, his own eyes glistening with unshed tears.

"Oh, my dear **Yousuf**," he whispered, his voice trembling, "I wish I had the answers that would take away your pain. I wish I could promise you that the world is kind, that people do not hurt each other, and that justice always prevails. But the truth is, wars are seldom fought for justice or humanity—they are waged for power, greed, and control. Leaders, blinded by ambition, forget that behind every statistic of war lies a shattered home, a grieving mother, a child robbed of a future."

Tears began to stream down his wrinkled cheeks, and as **Yousuf** sobbed into his chest, the other children in the room, overwhelmed by the pain in his voice, began to cry as well. The room was filled with the quiet sounds of sorrow, a symphony of innocent souls mourning for a world they could not yet understand.

One child, through tear-filled eyes, whispered, "**Great Grandpa**, do you think robots could run parliaments and assemblies one day? Could AI-driven leaders stop the production of weapons of mass destruction and guide humanity away from annihilation?"

The **old man** wiped his tears, took a deep breath, and looked at them with all the wisdom his years had given him.

"Technology, my dear ones, is like a sword—it can either protect or destroy, depending on whose hands wield it. AI has the potential to process vast amounts of data, make unbiased decisions, and remove human emotions from governance. But here's the question: Do we truly want a world devoid of human conscience? A world where decisions are made by logic alone, without compassion, without the warmth of understanding? Yes, AI might solve many problems—perhaps even curb corruption, stabilize economies, and predict crises before they occur. But at the same time, AI has no soul, no sense of morality beyond what we program into it. The real challenge is not whether robots can rule—it is whether we, as humans, can rule ourselves wisely enough to ensure we never need them to."

The **children** exchanged glances, deep in thought. Then, another question surfaced, one that sent a shiver down their spines.

"**Great Grandpa**, ***we read something that Albert Einstein said—that while we don't know what weapons World War III will be fought with, World War IV will be fought with sticks and stones. Does that mean the third world war will be so destructive that it will wipe out everything? Will it leave nothing behind but ruins, forcing humanity***

to start over, like our forefathers in the Stone Age? Is that what awaits us?"

At this, the old man's body shook, and his face contorted with grief. He could no longer hold back his sorrow, and tears fell freely from his eyes. "Oh, my dear children," he whispered, "Einstein was warning us. He saw the path we were treading and feared that if we continued down it, we would bring about our destruction. The truth is, war has never truly ended—it only changes form. Today, battles are not just fought with guns and bombs, but with economic sanctions, cyber warfare, and misinformation. The weapons of the future may not only be nuclear, but biological, digital, and psychological. But hear me well—if mankind chooses war over peace, if hatred outweighs wisdom, then yes, we may find ourselves back in the Stone Age, with nothing left but regret."

The **childre**n wept openly now, their fragile hearts unable to bear the weight of his words. One of them, voice trembling, finally whispered the most heartbreaking question of all.

"**Great Grandpa**, does that mean our children have no future? No hope for a world of peace, love, and dreams? Are we destined to inherit a world on the brink of destruction, where everything we cherish will vanish in the flames of war?" Will we face a new age of terror, like the age of dinosaurs, where survival is ruled by fear and chaos?

The great-grandfather's entire body trembled, and he hugged **Yousuf** and the **other children** tightly, his own sobs joining theirs. He held them as though he could shield them from all the darkness in the world, as though his embrace alone could mend the shattered pieces of their innocence. And then, when he finally found his voice again, it was strong, filled with an unshakable resolve.

"No, my dear ones. You must never believe that. The future is not written in stone—it is shaped by the choices we make today. Yes, there are wars. Yes, there is suffering. But there is also kindness, courage, and the unbreakable human spirit. History is not just a story of destruction; it is also a story of resilience, of rebuilding, of hope rising from the ashes. Your generation has the power to choose differently. You can demand leaders who value peace over power, who build bridges instead of walls. You can choose knowledge over ignorance, unity over division, love over hate. The future is not doomed, my children—it is waiting for hands like yours to shape it into something beautiful."

The great-grandfather then stood up, his frail frame now filled with a quiet strength. His voice, though choked with emotion, carried a message of unwavering hope.

"Let your hearts never be hardened by the cruelty of the world. Be the light where there is darkness, the voice of justice where there is silence. If you want a world free of war, be its peacemakers. If you want a world of love, be its givers. If you want a future worth living, start building it today. The greatest battle you will ever fight is not with weapons but with your own conscience. The greatest victory is not in conquering lands, but in conquering hatred within. The world is not lost yet, my dear children, as long as there are souls like yours willing to heal it."

A hush fell over the room, but this time, it was not the silence of fear—it was the silence of realization. **Yousuf** and the other children sat straighter, a newfound determination flickering in their eyes.

Perhaps the world was broken, but it was not beyond repair. And perhaps, just perhaps, they were the ones who would mend it.

Session Six

The Great-Grandfather Diaries: Fact, Fiction, and Future Dreams

Wisdom of a Great Grandfather: Reflections on Life

"A Wonderful Surprise for Great Grandpa"

After a long wait, Saturday finally arrived. The three **children** were excited, eager to resume their cherished conversations with their beloved **great-grandpa**. It was a beautiful morning—the golden sunlight bathed everything in warmth, a gentle breeze carried the fresh, earthy scent of last night's drizzle, and the cheerful chatter of birds filled the air. Butterflies flitted gracefully across the open sky, adding to the moment's magic.

Great Grandpa, as always, was ready for their cherished morning gathering, his fingers wrapped around his favorite black coffee mug, the rich aroma swirling around him like an old companion. He had chosen the perfect spot in the spacious drawing room—a place where comfort met elegance. Settling into a sleek IKEA armchair, he took a deep breath, letting the warmth of the golden morning seep into his soul.

The room was bathed in the soft glow of the early sun, its golden rays streaming through the tall, flowing curtains, casting a dance of light and shadow across the space. A regal blue velvet sofa stretched invitingly, its plush cushions promising comfort and long, heartfelt conversations. Beneath it, a breathtaking Persian carpet, alive with intricate patterns of crimson, sapphire, and gold, spread like a grand tapestry, each thread woven with artistry. The golden curtains swayed gently with the morning breeze, carrying the sweet, floral fragrance of blooming roses from the front yard garden.

Above, a magnificent white chandelier shimmered in the daylight, its crystals catching the morning sun, scattering tiny rainbows across the ceiling. Nearby, the grand dining table stood with quiet sophistication, its polished wooden surface gleaming under the natural light, surrounded by six elegantly carved chairs with silk cushions that added a touch of grace and refinement. A delicate porcelain vase sat at the center, cradling fresh lilies and roses, their fragrance mingling with the aroma of freshly brewed coffee and warm, buttery croissants from the kitchen.

But the true soul of the room was its walls, transformed by **Grandma's** artistic magic. Vivid landscapes, serene natural scenes, and abstract masterpieces breathed life into the space, each brushstroke infused with her passion and dedication. Some paintings captured the golden embrace of the rising sun over misty fields, while others depicted a tranquil morning by a peaceful lake. The abstract ones, bold and full of imagination, invited endless interpretations and musings. Each piece was a window into her creative soul, a testament to her tireless effort to bring beauty and freshness into their home.

The morning air was crisp, filled with the sounds of birds chirping just outside the windows. A gentle rustling of leaves added a soothing melody to the serene ambiance. As **Great Grandpa** took a slow sip of his coffee, he smiled, knowing that soon, the room would be filled with laughter, chatter, and stories, weaving another beautiful moment into the tapestry of their lives.

It was a morning filled with joy and anticipation, a day unlike any other for their beloved **Great Grandpa**. The **children** arrived, dressed in bright, beautifully colored outfits, their faces glowing with excitement. In their small hands, they carried a delicate bouquet of fresh roses, their petals kissed by the morning dew, filling the air with a soft, sweet fragrance.

With wide smiles, they called out in unison, "Good morning, **Great Grandpa**!"

His face lit up instantly, his eyes twinkling with delight. He opened his arms wide, his voice warm and affectionate as he welcomed them, "A very good morning to all of you, my dears!"

But little did he know, this morning held an even greater surprise. For the past five days, the children had been keeping a wonderful secret, their whispers and giggles filling the house as they carefully planned this special moment. Hidden away in their bedroom was a tiny, living treasure—one they had eagerly waited to present.

As the moment arrived, **Mariyam**, the eldest, stepped forward, her hands cradling something wrapped in a soft, white satin cloth. Her heart raced with excitement as she carefully unfolded the fabric, revealing a tiny, breathtakingly **beautiful kitten—Lucy**. Her fur was a striking blend of black, white, and orange, her eyes wide with curiosity, her little paws twitching as if she already sensed the love that awaited her.

"Surprise, **Great Grandpa**!" the children cheered, their voices bursting with joy.

For a moment, he simply stared, his eyes widening in astonishment. Then, as if drawn by an invisible thread of affection, his hands reached out, trembling slightly, to hold the tiny kitten. He gently scooped her into his embrace, his heart swelling with emotion. As he stroked her soft fur, he felt an unexpected warmth spread through him—a warmth that only love and companionship could bring.

His voice, thick with gratitude, trembled as he spoke, "My dear little ones, this is the most wonderful gift I could have ever imagined. You have not just given me a pet—you have given me a new companion, a new listener for my stories, and perhaps even another little one to ask me endless questions!"

The children burst into laughter, their hearts full, knowing they had given their **Great Grandpa** something truly special. He smiled, looking around at their bright, eager faces. Then, with a playful glint in his eyes, he made a loving declaration.

"From today, I don't just have three **great-grandchildren**—I have four! And this little one," he said, gently lifting **Lucy**, "is now a part of our family, a part of my heart."

And so, **Lucy** was no longer just a surprise gift—she was a new member of their home, a tiny bundle of joy that would bring warmth, laughter, and endless storytelling into their lives.

Their laughter echoed in the room, and their eyes sparkled with anticipation. They were ready to dive into another delightful session of stories, wisdom, and laughter with their **Great-grandpa**, their favorite storyteller, mentor, and friend.

With time, the great-grandchildren had grown sharper, their curious minds now fine-tuned like seasoned interviewers. They had mastered the art of rapid-fire questioning, much like the anchors of Times of India, BBC, NBC, CBS, ABC, and Fox, grilling world leaders and experts with relentless enthusiasm. But today, their subject wasn't a politician or a scientist—it was their very own **Great Grandpa**!

For him, answering their endless stream of questions was no easy task. It was like stepping into a high-stakes press conference where every answer had to be backed by wisdom, experience, and a touch of humor. But if there was anyone ready for the challenge, it was **Great Grandpa**—the walking treasure chest of knowledge and life experiences. His years of learning, staying updated with newspapers, science magazines, TV programs, and journals, had made him a man of great wisdom. No doubt, he had always been sharp, quick-witted, and effortlessly intelligent when it came to handling any situation. His sharp memory, fueled by a healthy and joyful lifestyle, made him the perfect candidate for this grand Q&A session.

This time, the children had strategically planned their questions, carefully noting them down in their diaries. They had divided them into five thrilling categories:

1. Curiosity About the Past – Digging into **Great Grandpa's** childhood adventures and forgotten stories.
2. Lessons from Life – Extracting pearls of wisdom from his long journey.
3. Family and Love – Unraveling the most heartwarming moments of his life.
4. Imagination and Fun – Testing how creative and playful he could still be!
5. Wisdom and the Future – Seeking guidance for the paths they had yet to walk.

The stage was set, the anticipation was high, and the **great-grandchildren** were ready with their notebooks and eager eyes. Would **Great Grandpa** be able to satisfy their boundless curiosity? Would his answers spark laughter, amazement, or even more questions?

With a smile, **Great Grandpa** leaned forward, ready to embrace the challenge. "Alright, little reporters," he chuckled, "Fire away!"

And just like that, the grand Q&A session began—a battle of wits, wisdom, and wonder, where every answer carried a story, and every question brought them closer to the heart of their beloved **Great Grandpa**.

The Ultimate Q&A Show with Great Grandpa

Maryam, always the most eager of the bunch, stepped forward, clutching her diary like a seasoned journalist about to grill a world leader. She adjusted her imaginary glasses, cleared her throat, and with a mischievous grin, launched a rapid-fire round of questions.

"**Great Grandpa**, could you please answer me honestly?" she said, her eyes twinkling.

Great Grandpa chuckled. "My dear, at my age, honesty is the only policy. I have no energy left to make up stories!" he said with a wink.

And so, the questioning began!

1. "Great Grandpa, ***what was the happiest memory of your childhood?"***

Great Grandpa's eyes sparkled with nostalgia. "Oh, that's easy! The day I won a whole bag of sweets in a marble game. I felt like the king of the world—until your Great-Great Grandma found out and made me share with my siblings. That was the day I learned the meaning of 'easy come, easy go!'"

2. *"Did you ever have a pet when you were a child? What was it like?"*

"Yes! I had a parrot named **Mithu**. He was a chatterbox, much like you kids! He could mimic my father's voice so well that I once got scolded for something Mithu actually said. I still believe that bird had a wicked sense of humor!"

3. *"What were your favorite games when you were our age? Were they as fun as Ludo and chess?"*

Great Grandpa laughed. "We played all sorts of games—marbles, hopscotch, kite-flying, and a wild game called 'steal-the-mango'... though that one wasn't exactly legal!" He winked. "And believe me, dodging an angry orchard owner was more thrilling than any game of Ludo!"

4. *"Did you ever do something mischievous when you were a kid and get caught?"*

Great Grandpa rubbed his chin, pretending to think. "Oh, I was a saint... except for that one time when I tied a fake snake to my teacher's chair. The scream he let out is still echoing somewhere in the universe. I got caught, of course, and my punishment? Writing 'I will not prank my teacher' 100 times. Guess what? I wrote it only 50 times and told him the ink ran out!"

The **children** burst into laughter.

5. "How was school different when you were young? Did you have homework like we do?"

"Different? Oh yes! We had no computers, no fancy projectors—just a blackboard and a teacher with a stick! And homework? Oh, we had plenty! The only difference is, we couldn't ask Google for answers. We had to actually use our brains!"

6. ***"If you could go back in time and give your younger self one piece of advice, what would it be?"***

Great Grandpa leaned forward with a wise smile. "I'd tell my younger self," 'Don't rush to grow up!' Childhood is like an ice cream on a hot day—enjoy it before it melts!"

7. ***"What is the biggest lesson life has taught you?"***

He sighed thoughtfully. "Life has taught me that happiness isn't about how much you have, but how much you appreciate it. Even a simple cup of tea tastes better when shared with loved ones."

8. ***"Have you ever faced a difficult time that made you stronger? How did you overcome it?"***

"Oh, many times! Life is like a cricket match—sometimes you hit a six, and sometimes you get bowled out. But I learned that every failure teaches you something valuable. I overcame tough times with patience, faith, and a good sense of humor!"

9. ***"What is the secret to a happy and long life?"***

Great Grandpa's eyes twinkled as he stretched his arms wide, a warm smile spreading across his face. "The secret?" he chuckled. "Laugh until your belly aches, savor every bite of good food, keep your mind curious like a child's, and never let worries steal your sleep! And, of course," he added with a wink, "having mischievous great-grandkids like you keeps my heart young and my days full of adventure!"

The **children** clapped and cheered, completely in awe of their **Great Grandpa's** wisdom, humor, and incredible stories.

Mariyam grinned. "Wow, **Great Grandpa**! You should be on TV!"

He chuckled. "Well, my dear, who needs TV when I have the best live audience right here?"

And with that, the rapid-fire session continued, filling the room with laughter, love, and the magic of storytelling.

The Grand Q&A Battle Continues!

After **Mariyam's** rapid-fire round, the next ball was in **Ibrahim's** court! Being the smart one, he stepped forward like a champion bowler, ready to bowl out his **Great Grandpa** with a series of tricky, thought-provoking questions.

"Great Grandpa, I expect only genuine answers! No dodging, okay?" **Ibrahim** warned with a playful smirk.

Great Grandpa laughed, leaning back comfortably. "Oh, young man, at my age, I don't have the energy to make up fake stories. Go ahead, let's see what you've got!"

And so, the Q&A battle continued!

1. ***"If you could change one thing about the world today, what would it be?"***

Great Grandpa sighed, stroking his chin. "I would erase greed from people's hearts. Imagine a world where no one was selfish—where the rich actually shared with the poor, and everyone cared for one another. Then, I wouldn't have to watch the news and get upset every morning!"

Ibrahim nodded, impressed. "That's deep, **Great Grandpa**. But what if you had to change something fun?"

Great Grandpa grinned. "Alright, then! I'd make chocolate healthy so you kids could eat it for breakfast, lunch, and dinner without your parents scolding you!"

The children erupted in cheers. "Now, that's a great idea!"

2. ***"How did you meet Great Grandma? Was it love at first sight?"***

Great Grandpa chuckled, his eyes twinkling with nostalgia. "Oh, it was love at first sight… at least for me! She, on the other hand, took her sweet time deciding whether I was worth it!"

The kids gasped. "Really? What did you do to impress her?"

"Oh, I tried everything! I wrote poetry—terrible poetry, by the way. I even learned to cook her favorite dish, but I accidentally set the kitchen on fire! But in the end, she liked me not for my talents, but for my persistence and kindness. And that's when I learned—love isn't about grand gestures, it's about being there, always."

Ibrahim clapped. "That's smooth, **Great Grandpa.** You could give love lessons!"

3. ***"What is the most beautiful thing about having a family?"***

Great Grandpa smiled warmly. "Family is like a tree. Some branches grow in different directions, but we all stay connected at the roots. No matter how far you go in life, your family will always be there to give you shade and support when you need it. And the best part? With each new generation, the tree grows bigger and stronger!"

The children looked at each other, feeling a deep sense of love for their **Great Grandpa.**

4. ***"What were our parents like when they were kids? Were they naughty or well-behaved?"***

Great Grandpa laughed so hard that his shoulders shook. "Your parents? Oh, they were little troublemakers! Don't let their serious faces fool you. Your dad once tried to convince me that his homework got eaten by a squirrel, and your mom—oh, she was the queen of sneaking extra cookies when no one was looking!"

Ibrahim's jaw dropped. "Wait, so they were just like us?"

"Oh, much worse! But that's the beauty of life—naughty kids grow up to become responsible parents, and then they get to deal with little mischief-makers like you!"

The children giggled, loving this new insight into their parents' past.

5. ***"What is your favorite thing about being a Great Grandpa?"***

Great Grandpa's eyes softened. "My favorite thing? You kids! You bring energy, joy, and endless curiosity into my life. Every day with you is a new adventure, and I wouldn't trade it for anything in the world."

The kids smiled, touched by his words. "We love you, **Great Grandpa!"**

6. ***"Do you think we are different from how children were in your time?"***

Great Grandpa nodded. "Oh, absolutely! You kids are smarter, faster, and have the whole world in your pockets with these smartphones! But you also get bored too quickly. Back in my day, we could turn a stick and a piece of string into hours of entertainment!"

Ibrahim laughed. “That’s true! We do get bored fast. So what’s better—your childhood or ours?”

Great Grandpa grinned. “Oh, each era has its magic! We had simpler joys, you have grander possibilities. The trick is to enjoy whatever time you’re in to the fullest.”

7. ***"If you could have any superpower, what would it be and why?"***

Great Grandpa tapped his chin. "Hmm... I’d choose the power to eat as much biryani as I want without gaining weight!"

The kids burst out laughing.

"But seriously," he continued, "I’d choose the power to heal people’s hearts—not just from sickness, but from sadness. Imagine a world where no one felt lonely or broken. Now, that would be a true superpower!"

The children were silent for a moment, amazed by his wisdom.

8. ***"If you could travel back in time to any period in history, where would you go?"***

Great Grandpa’s face lit up. "Oh, I’d love to visit ancient civilizations! Maybe walk through the great libraries of Alexandria, meet Leonardo da Vinci, or witness the Taj Mahal being built! But only if I could take a good bed with me—those stone benches in history didn’t look comfortable!"

Ibrahim laughed. “**Great Grandpa**, you’re hilarious!”

"Well," **Great Grandpa** said with a wink, "A long life teaches you two things—wisdom and the importance of a good mattress!"

The Grand Finale

The children clapped excitedly. "That was amazing, **Great Grandpa!** You should be on a talk show!"

Great Grandpa chuckled. "Who needs a talk show when I have the best audience right here?"

And with that, the laughter and stories continued, making this day one to remember—a perfect blend of wisdom, humor, and love that only a **Great Grandpa** could provide.

Yousuf's Turn: The Trickiest Questions Yet!

After the rapid-fire rounds from **Maryam** and **Ibrahim**, it was now curious **Yousuf**'s turn. He smiled mischievously, rubbing his hands like a detective about to crack a tough case.

"Great Grandpa, get ready! My questions are tricky!" he declared.

Great Grandpa chuckled, folding his arms. "Oh, **Yousuf,** my dear, I've seen more tricky questions in life than all your school exams combined! But I promised to answer honestly, so go ahead—bowl your best!"

And with that, the Q&A battle continued!

1. ***"If you could live in a storybook, which one would it be?"***

Great Grandpa tapped his chin thoughtfully. "Hmm… I'd choose **Alice in Wonderland**."

"***Why***?" **Yousuf** asked, surprised.

"Because it's a place where the impossible happens every second! Imagine sitting with a talking cat, drinking tea that makes you shrink, and playing chess with living pieces. But the best part? There's no homework in Wonderland!"

The kids laughed, nodding in agreement.

"Though," **Great Grandpa** added with a wink, "I'd make one change—I'd bring a comfortable armchair. All that running around would be too much for my old legs!"

2. ***"Do you believe in magic? Have you ever experienced something magical in life?"***

Great Grandpa's eyes twinkled. "Oh, I absolutely believe in magic! But not the kind with wands and spells."

Yousuf leaned in curiously. "Then what kind of magic?"

"The magic of love, kindness, and moments that take your breath away. Like when I first held your Great Grandma's hand, or when I saw your father take his first steps, or when I heard you call me '**Great Grandpa**' for the first time. That, my dear, is real magic!"

Yousuf *grinned mischievously. "That's beautiful,* ***Great Grandpa**! **But no flying carpets or Aladdin's magic lamp?"***

Great Grandpa chuckled, his eyes twinkling. "No flying carpets, my dear, but who needs one when your imagination can soar beyond the stars? A magic lamp grants just three wishes—but your mind? It holds endless possibilities!"

3. ***"If Lucy, our kitten, could talk, what do you think she would say to us?"***

Great Grandpa's eyes twinkled with mischief as he leaned in, lowering his voice as if revealing a grand secret. "Oh, she'd probably sigh in relief and say, 'Finally! Someone understands me!'"

The kids erupted into giggles, eager for more.

Great Grandpa chuckled and continued, now imitating Lucy's voice with exaggerated drama. "She'd say, 'First of all, stop calling me cute—I am a *fearless* tiger in disguise! I rule this house, and you are my loyal subjects!'"

The children clapped and laughed as Lucy, as if on cue, stretched lazily, flicking her tail like a true queen.

"And of course," **Great Grandpa** added, rubbing his chin thoughtfully, "she would demand, 'Now, about that fridge—someone open it already! I *know* you're hiding the good stuff in there, and I am *tired* of waiting!'"

The kids howled with laughter, nodding in agreement, as if they, too, had seen Lucy eyeing the fridge with suspicion.

Then, with a sly grin, **Great Grandpa** raised a finger and added, "And, without a doubt, she'd lecture us all, saying, 'Listen up, humans—no Tattoos, no Alcohol, no Drugs, no Smoking and no Tobacco! I don't like them, and I *definitely* don't take them! "Stay elegant and wise—just like a true gentleman or lady should!"

That was it—everyone burst into laughter, glancing at Lucy, who now lounged with an air of royal approval, her whiskers twitching as if to say, *Exactly. Finally, someone gets it!*

4. ***"What dreams do you have for us, your great-grandchildren?"***

Great Grandpa's face softened. "My dream for you is simple—I want you to be good human beings. I don't care if you become doctors, engineers, artists, or astronauts. What matters is that you are kind, honest, and always ready to help someone in need."

Yousuf nodded thoughtfully. "That's a great dream, **Great Grandpa."**

"And also," **Great Grandpa** added with a twinkle in his eye, "I dream that you kids will one day let me win at Ludo and carrom, Just once!"

The children giggled. "No way, **Great Grandpa!** You're too good!"

5. ***"How can we make sure we live a good and meaningful life like you?"***

Great Grandpa leaned forward, lowering his voice as if sharing a great secret. "The trick is simple: Always keep learning, always stay curious, and always find reasons to laugh. And never forget—life is too short to waste on being angry over small things."

The children listened carefully, feeling the weight of his wisdom.

"And," he added, grinning, "never say no to dessert. It keeps the heart happy!"

6. ***"What do you think the world will be like when we grow up?"***

Great Grandpa sighed, looking into the distance. "The world will be faster, smarter, and maybe even have flying cars! But the real question is—will it be kinder?"

Yousuf tilted his head. ***"What do you mean?"***

"No matter how much technology advances, the most important thing is that people remain compassionate. If you grow up to be someone who spreads kindness, then the world will be better—no matter how many robots or space trips we have!"

7. ***"What is the one thing we should never forget, no matter how much the world changes?"***

Great Grandpa smiled. "Never forget where you came from. Never forget your values. And never forget the people who love you."

Yousuf nodded seriously. "That's a good answer."

"Oh, and also," **Great Grandpa** added with a chuckle, "never forget to double-check before sending a text message. One wrong emoji can turn a serious message into a joke!"

The kids burst into laughter.

8. ***"If we ever feel lost or unsure about life, what advice would you give us to find our way?"***

Great Grandpa's voice became gentle. "Whenever you feel lost, remember three things: One, take a deep breath—calmness helps you think better. Two, talk to someone you trust—never keep your worries locked inside. And three, always trust that no matter how dark the night, the sun will rise again."

The room fell silent for a moment as the children absorbed his words.

"And if all else fails," he added with a mischievous grin, "come to me! I may be old, but I still give the best advice… and the best snacks!"

The children laughed and hugged their **Great Grandpa,** feeling grateful for his wisdom, his humor, and most of all, his love.

And so, the Great Q&A Battle came to an end, but the lessons and laughter they shared would stay in their hearts forever.

But the Kitten **Lucy** so far sitting in the cozy lap of **Great Grandpa** was still thinking about continuing the session for some more time and not ready to come down from the lap. When **Maryam** tried to take her in her lap refused to come out and started crying. **Great Grandpa** could understand the possible reason and expected she might be having some questions to be asked. She could understand the only language of **Yousuf**, therefore **Yousuf** came forward and asked her any question you too ask? She started murmuring to Mao Mao, **Yousuf** could understand her language and explained to everybody including the **Great Grandpa** that she was asking about tomorrow's picnic program? They explained that tomorrow is the picnic in Redwood National Park, San Francisco,

California and they will also take her there for a trip and fun. Only then did she leap off **Great Grandpa**'s lap, giggling as she joined the other children in their play. With that, today's lively session came to a cheerful close, making way for a delicious lunch and the exciting preparations for tomorrow's grand picnic.

Session Seven

Wisdom of a Great Grandfather: Reflections on Life

In Their Eyes: Conversations with the Next Generation

"Harmony in Devotion: Understanding the Soul of Worship Across Faiths"

This morning was wonderful. Moderate Cold breeze was blowing and the front yard garden flowers were in bloom. Colorful roses gave a wonderful rainbow look with the fragrance of roses, jasmine, and lily. The whole sky was covered with clouds of different colors. Colorful Birds were chatting on the flower stems and leaves. Honey bees are busily sucking the nectar of roses and Jasmine and Lilies. Sunrise is about to take place. The darkness of night is slowly converting to cloudy lights. Moments are beautiful to enjoy from nature. Poets can draw a very romantic poem and Ghazal on the beauty of the present nature.

After his morning prayer, **Great Grandpa** went for the morning walk with his favorite stick and white kits and was soon about to return.

When he returned, **Great Grandpa** went to the kitchen for his black coffee in his favorite black mug. He is now back in the family room, sitting on the armchair, enjoying his sips of coffee. He is waiting for the **great-grandchildren** to come down, and as usual, he starts a new session of conversation on different topics of life. **Great Grandpa** is well prepared and updated to address the questions properly within the range of the children's brains.

The morning sun cast a golden glow over the garden, with a gentle breeze rustling through the leaves, carrying the sweet scent of blooming flowers. Sensing the perfect weather, **Great-Grandpa** decided to hold today's storytelling session right in the heart of the garden, where nature itself could be part of their joy.

As the morning sun cast gentle rays through the curtains, a familiar symphony began to unfold. The soft, insistent "Mao Mao" of Lucy echoed down the staircase, heralding the imminent arrival of the great-grandchildren. With a playful way, Lucy trotted ahead, her excitement palpable as she reached Great-Grandpa, playfully nuzzling and pawing at his feet, seeking his affectionate touch.

Moments later, the house resonated with the joyous clamor of youthful voices. The children descended the stairs like a jubilant parade, each step filled with exuberance. Their laughter intertwined, creating a melody of familial love that filled every corner of the home.

Emerging one by one, they showcased their unique styles—each outfit carefully chosen, each hairstyle a testament to their playful rivalry, as if silently competing to outshine one another. Though breakfast had long passed, their pockets jingled with the delightful secret of roasted dry fruits, a clandestine stash for mid-morning indulgence. With careful hands, they carried an extra plate, laden with treats, destined for their beloved **Great-Grandpa.**

This intergenerational bond, rich with shared moments and traditions, exemplifies the profound connection between great-grandparents and great-grandchildren. Such relationships are invaluable, fostering mutual respect, love, and a deep sense of belonging. Grandparents often serve as pillars of wisdom and stability, enriching their grandchildren's lives with stories, guidance, and unwavering support.

In this beautiful tapestry of love and tradition, the family discovered more than just fleeting moments of joy—they found a living bridge between generations, where the past and future intertwined through shared experiences and unwavering affection. Even **Lucy,** with her boundless energy, moved among them like one of the children, mirroring their excitement with playful enthusiasm.

Then, as if guided by an unspoken rhythm, they burst into song—a melody of pure joy filling the air. Laughter danced in their voices, their feet tapping in perfect harmony as they rushed toward him, with **Lucy** bounding alongside them. Their chorus rose in jubilant unison:

"GOOD MORNING, GREAT-GRANDPA!"

Their energy was infectious, sending waves of laughter cascading through the garden, turning it into a haven of pure, unfiltered joy. It felt as though the morning itself had paused to bask in the magic of this moment, the sunlight dancing through the leaves in quiet applause.

Great-grandpa, his heart swelling with love, couldn't contain his delight. His rich, hearty laughter blended seamlessly with theirs, echoing through the air like a song of happiness. With arms outstretched, he gathered them all in a warm, all-encompassing embrace, as if trying to capture the very essence of life in that single, precious moment. Then, with a twinkle in his eyes, he lifted his beloved **Lucy**, pressing a tender kiss to her head before nestling her gently in his lap—his little companion in this beautiful dance of love and togetherness.

For a man on the brink of completing a century, these were the moments that made time stand still—where age melted away, and he felt just as young and vibrant as the little ones gathered around him. With a twinkle in his eyes, he welcomed them warmly and, as was tradition, settled into his favorite armchair. The rich aroma of freshly brewed coffee swirled around him as he took slow, thoughtful sips, savoring both the drink and the delightful company before him.

But today, something was different. Breaking from the usual pattern, little **Yousuf** bravely stepped forward, his eyes shining with excitement. He cleared his throat and, with a sense of purpose, asked **Great-Grandpa** for permission to begin the session.

Intrigued, **Great-Grandpa** nodded approvingly. "Go ahead, my little philosopher! And what grand topic have you all chosen for today?"

A brief hush fell over the group as they huddled together, whispering and exchanging glances, their young minds quietly deliberating. Then, as if reaching a silent agreement, they turned back to him, their voices united in a single declaration:

"Today's topic is... EXPLORING THE PURPOSE OF LIFE!"

Great-grandpa raised an eyebrow, momentarily taken aback. Of all the subjects they could have chosen, this was by far the deepest—and certainly the most complex for children of their age. But looking at their eager faces, he knew this would be unlike any session they had ever had.

A conversation like this would not just challenge them—it would challenge him, too.

With a knowing smile, he set down his coffee cup, leaned forward slightly, and said, "Well then, my dear ones... let's begin."

Yousuf, with his usual curiosity, wasted no time and jumped straight into his questions. His eyes sparkled with the excitement of unraveling one of life's greatest mysteries.

"**Great Grandpa,** ***what is the ultimate purpose of life?"***

Great-grandpa smiled, taking a deep breath as he leaned back in his chair. "Ah, my dear **Yousuf**, that is the question mankind has been asking for centuries! The ultimate purpose of life is not the same for everyone—it is like a journey where each person must find their path. Some believe it is about seeking happiness, others say it is about serving others, and some think it is about worshipping the Creator. In the end, life is like a river—it keeps flowing, and along the way, we must learn, grow, and leave behind something meaningful."

Yousuf: ***How do different faiths guide us in understanding this profound aspect of life?***

Great Grandpa: "My dear **Yousuf**, this is the question that has puzzled humans since the beginning of time. Different religions and philosophies offer different answers, but at the heart of them all is the idea that life has meaning beyond just survival. As for example:

- **In Islam**, the purpose of life is to worship Allah, do good deeds, and prepare for the Hereafter.

  In Islam, worship (ʿibādah - عبادة) is a comprehensive concept that goes beyond rituals like prayer and fasting. It encompasses every action, intention, and thought that is done sincerely for the sake of Allah (God), in accordance with His guidance.

  Worship in Islam is not limited to specific religious acts; rather, it includes everything a person does with sincerity to seek Allah's pleasure—whether through formal acts of devotion or daily actions aligned with His commands.

  The Quran states: "And I did not create the jinn and mankind except to worship Me." *(Surah Adh-Dhariyat 51:56).* This verse signifies that worship is the ultimate purpose of human existence.

Types of Worship in Islam

- Ritual Worship (Ibadat) – Acts of Direct Devotion
  These include prescribed religious duties:
  - Salah (Prayer) – The five daily prayers.
  - Sawm (Fasting) – Especially in Ramadan.
  - Zakat (Charity) – Obligatory almsgiving.
  - Hajj (Pilgrimage) – For those who can afford it.
- General Worship – Everyday Acts Done for Allah's Sake
  - Earning a lawful livelihood (Halal Rizq).
  - Being kind to family and neighbors.
  - Helping the poor and needy.

- Seeking knowledge for the benefit of society.
- Maintaining honesty and integrity in all dealings.
- Avoiding sins and harmful actions.

The Prophet Muhammad (PBUH) said: *"Actions are but by intentions, and every person will have only what they intended."*
(Sahih al-Bukhari, Sahih Muslim)

This means that even everyday actions—if done with the right intention—become acts of worship.

Conditions of True Worships in different faiths

Conditions of True Worship in Islam

- Sincerity (Ikhlas) – Worship should be solely for Allah (God).
- Correctness (Muwafaqah) – It must follow the teachings of the Quran and Sunnah.
- Love and Devotion – Worship should be done with reverence, love, and hope in Allah's mercy.

Conclusion:

In Islam, worship is not confined to mosques or rituals; it is a way of life. Every act—whether prayer, charity, or even a simple smile—can be worshiped if done with sincerity and in accordance with Allah's guidance.

"Journeying through the world's faiths to uncover their unique insights into the profound mystery of life."

"Exploring how Christianity, Judaism, Hinduism, Buddhism, Sikhism, and even Atheism offer unique windows into understanding this profound mystery of life."

- **Christianity** teaches that the purpose of life is to love God and others, following the teachings of Jesus Christ. The Bible says, *'Love the Lord your God with all your heart and with all your soul and with all your mind.'* (Matthew 22:37)
- **Judaism** teaches that life is about fulfilling God's commandments and bringing justice and righteousness into the world. The Torah emphasizes the idea of *Tikkun Olam*—repairing the world through good actions.
- **Hinduism** believes in four main purposes of life: **Dharma** (duty), **Artha** (prosperity), **Kama** (desires), and **Moksha** (liberation from the cycle of rebirth).
- **Buddhism** teaches that the purpose of life is to end suffering and reach enlightenment through wisdom, meditation, and ethical living.
- **Sikhism** believes that life is about remembering and serving God, living honestly, and helping humanity. Guru Nanak taught, *'Truth is high, but higher still is truthful living.'*
- **Atheists** (not believing in God) - generally believe that the ultimate purpose of life is not dictated by a divine being but is instead something each individual must define for themselves. Without belief in a higher power or an afterlife, many atheists find meaning in personal fulfillment, relationships, knowledge, and contributing to the well-being of others and society.

"So you see, my dear ones, while the paths may be different, the goal is the same—to live a life of meaning, purpose, and goodness."

Yousuf: ***"Great Grandpa, I truly believe that all faiths carry the same message of peace and compassion. But if that's true, why is the***

world filled with so much hatred, ethnic conflicts, and even mass killings in the name of religion? It seems like more lives have been lost in faith-related violence than in ordinary wars. Why do people fight over something that was meant to unite them?"

Great Grandpa: *"Yousuf,* *my dear, you've asked a question that has troubled humanity for centuries. It's true that all faiths preach love, kindness, and peace, yet history is stained with conflicts in the name of religion. But let me tell you something—faith itself is not the problem; the way people interpret and misuse it is."*

"You see, faith was meant to bring people together, to give them hope and purpose. But throughout history, rulers, politicians, and power-hungry individuals have twisted its message for their own gain. They have divided people by making them believe that their way is the only way, that others are enemies. And once fear and hatred take root, they spread like wildfire."

"Yes, faith-based conflicts have taken many lives, but the truth is, most wars are not truly about faith. They are about power, land, resources, and control. Faith is often just the banner under which these battles are fought. Even today, we see people using religion as a tool to manipulate and divide, but if we look closely, we'll find that greed, politics, and personal interests are the real driving forces behind much of the violence."

"However, remember this, ***Yousuf:*** *for every act of hatred committed in the name of faith, there are countless acts of kindness, love, and unity inspired by it. The media shows us conflicts, but in quiet corners of the world, people of different faiths help and care for each other every day. It is up to us to carry the true message of faith—one of peace, compassion, and understanding."*

"So, never let hatred cloud your heart. Instead, be the kind of person who builds bridges, who sees humanity beyond labels, and who spreads light where others bring darkness. That is the greatest service you can do—not just for your faith, but for all of humankind."

Yousuf: Great Grandpa, *I believe that the core messages and commandments of all divine revelations must be the same since they come from the One and Only Creator. However, over time, these messages seem to have been altered or misinterpreted, sometimes for personal gain, especially by religious leaders who may have used them to maintain power or wealth. Could you help me understand this logically?*

Great Grandpa: That's a very thoughtful observation, Yousuf! You are absolutely right that the essence of all divine revelations remains the same because the Creator is One, and His guidance for humanity has always been based on truth, justice, and righteousness. However, history shows us that human interpretation and intervention have sometimes led to distortions.

There are a few logical reasons for this:

1. Power and Influence: Some religious leaders, rather than serving as humble guides, saw an opportunity to gain authority over people. By modifying interpretations of divine laws, they could establish systems that favored their control and influence.

2. Cultural and Political Influence: As societies evolved, rulers and influential figures sometimes altered religious teachings to align with their personal interests or political agendas. Instead of preserving the original commandments, they manipulated them to justify wars, taxation, or social structures that benefited the elite.

3. Loss of Original Texts: Many ancient scriptures were transmitted orally before being recorded in writing. Over generations, this sometimes led to unintentional changes, misinterpretations, or even deliberate alterations by those who sought to reshape religious laws according to their own needs.

4. Human Desires and Weaknesses: The true essence of divine commandments often calls for discipline, fairness, and selflessness. However, human nature can sometimes incline toward greed and materialism. This led some individuals to dilute the original teachings to make them more convenient or profitable.

That being said, **Yousuf**, the message of truth can never be entirely lost. The original teachings of the last and final revelation remain preserved, and those who sincerely seek knowledge and guidance can always find their way back to the true path. It is our responsibility to differentiate between genuine faith and human distortions, using logic, history, and divine wisdom to understand the truth.

Your curiosity is a sign of a strong and wise mind—keep questioning, keep seeking, and never accept anything blindly. True faith is built upon understanding, not just following traditions without thought!

Yousuf: ***"But Great-Grandpa, why do different religions and philosophies have different views on life's purpose?"***

Great-Grandpa chuckled, nodding in appreciation of the question. "That's because humans are diverse, my dear. Just as we speak different languages and wear different clothes, our beliefs and understanding of life also differ. Every religion and philosophy tries to answer the same question—Why are we here? What should we do? What happens after we die?—but they answer them in their way. Some focus on devotion to God, others on self-discovery, and some on making the world a better place. The beauty of life is that even with all these differences, the core message often remains the same—live with kindness, seek wisdom, and strive for goodness."

Yousuf: ***"How can one find meaning in life beyond material success?"***

Great-grandpa's eyes softened as he looked at the young faces before him. "Ah, my dear ones, the true meaning is never found in wealth, fame, or possessions. Those are just temporary joys. Real meaning comes from love, relationships, learning, and helping others. Imagine a person who owns all the treasures in the world but has no one to share them with—would he be happy? No. A fulfilled life is one where your heart is at peace, where you have made a difference in someone's life, and where you wake up every day with a purpose greater than yourself."

He leaned forward, his eyes gleaming with wisdom, and spoke in a voice both gentle and commanding. "Ah, now this is a question that touches the very soul! Many believe that wealth, fame, and power hold the key to happiness, but in truth, they are mere illusions. Real fulfillment doesn't come from what we accumulate—it comes from what we share, the lives we touch, and the goodness we leave behind."

My dear **Yousuf,** have you ever heard of Bill Gates, Melinda French Gates, Warren Buffett, MacKenzie Scott, Jeff Bezos, Sir Chris Hohn, Michael Bloomberg, George Soros, Azim Premji, Reed Hastings, and Ruth Gottesman? These are some of the most renowned and influential personalities on our planet—individuals who accumulated immense wealth through relentless effort, determination, and innovation.

But do you know what they discovered after amassing billions? They realized that true happiness doesn't come from having more money; it comes from making a difference in the lives of others. Despite all their success, they felt an emptiness in their hearts—a void that wealth alone could not fill. That's when they made a remarkable decision: instead of hoarding their riches, they chose to give back. They dedicated their fortunes to uplifting the less privileged, supporting global causes, and improving the lives of millions.

Look at them now—truly content, at peace, and fulfilled. They have found the real meaning of success, not in wealth, but in kindness, generosity, and service to humanity. These are the real greats of the world, **Yousuf.** Wealth means nothing if it does not bring peace to your heart and soul—

if it does not let you sleep soundly at night. True success is not in what you have, but in what you give.

All faiths, my dear **Yousuf**, teach us the same profound truth—one that echoes across time, cultures, and generations.

Wealth is not the purpose of life. It is merely a tool.

Whether you look at Islam, Christianity, Hinduism, Buddhism, Judaism, Sikhism or any other faith, they all emphasize the same lesson: true fulfillment comes not from accumulating riches but from sharing, giving, and uplifting others.

- **Islam teaches us:** True success is not in wealth but in righteousness. The Quran says, 'Indeed, the most noble of you in the sight of Allah is the most righteous of you.' (Surah Al-Hujurat 49:13). "The best among you are those who bring the greatest benefit to others." (Hadith)
- **Christianity reminds us:** "It is more blessed to give than to receive." (Acts 20:35).
- **Hinduism guides us:** "They alone live who live for others." (Swami Vivekananda). Worldly success is temporary, but spiritual wisdom leads to eternal peace.
- **Buddhism tells us:** warns against attachment to material things, as they lead to suffering."If you light a lamp for someone else, it will also brighten your path.".
- **Judaism instructs:** That meaning is found in a life lived with integrity, wisdom, and service to others rather than in the endless pursuit of wealth.**"**Charity and justice are more acceptable to the Lord than sacrifice." (Proverbs 21:3)
- **Sikhism:** Teaches that honest living and serving others bring true fulfillment.

The greatest figures in history—prophets, saints, scholars, and now even billionaires—have all realized this truth. Happiness is not in hoarding but in giving. Satisfaction is not in possessing but in serving.

So, **Yousuf**, remember this always: true wealth is not what you keep; it is what you give away that brings peace to your heart and soul.

Yousuf: ***"How does faith help in understanding life's purpose?"***

Great-grandpa: He took a deep sip of his coffee before answering. "Faith is like a lighthouse in the stormy sea of life—it gives direction, hope, and strength.

- **Islam** teaches that faith (Iman) gives peace and helps believers trust in God's plan.
- **Christianity** teaches that faith in God's love helps people endure hardships.
- **Judaism** sees faith as a covenant between God and His people, giving them a sense of duty and purpose.
- **Hinduism and Buddhism** emphasize faith in the law of karma—that our actions shape our future.
- **Sikhism** teaches that remembering God in every moment helps overcome difficulties.

"Faith reminds us that even in suffering, there is wisdom, and even in loss, there is hope."

Yousuf: ***"Why do people turn to religion when questioning their existence?"***

Great-Grandpa nodded. "Because religion provides answers that logic alone cannot. When people face loss, pain, or uncertainty, they want to know *why*—why do we suffer, why do we die, why do good people face hardship?

- **Islam** teaches that life is a test and that patience (sabr) brings great rewards.

- **Christianity** teaches that suffering has meaning and that faith in God brings comfort.
- **Judaism** sees the search for meaning as a fundamental human need, and religion serves as a guiding light, offering purpose, moral clarity, and a deep connection to God and community.
- **Buddhism** teaches that suffering is part of life and can be overcome through wisdom and inner peace.
- **Hinduism** believes in karma—that every action has consequences, and our suffering is a result of past deeds.
- **Sikhism** teaches that remembering God and serving others helps people rise above suffering.

"So, my dear ones, when people struggle with life's biggest questions, they turn to religion because it gives them a sense of belonging, a purpose, and a path forward."

Yousuf: ***"What if someone does not follow any religion? Can they still have a purpose in life?"***

Great-Grandpa smiled warmly. "Of course, my dear **Yousuf**. Religion is one way to find purpose, but it is not the only way. Some people find meaning in science, art, helping others, or simply living a good life.

- Many philosophers believe that purpose comes from within—that we create our own meaning through our choices.
- Some scientists find purpose in exploring the mysteries of the universe.
- Many humanists believe that purpose comes from making the world a better place.

"In the end, a purposeful life is one where you wake up every morning with a reason to move forward—whether that reason comes from faith, love, curiosity, or the desire to create something beautiful."

Great Grandpa looked at them with deep affection. "The most important thing, my dear ones, is to live with kindness, seek knowledge, and never stop asking questions—because that is how we truly understand the purpose of life."

For a moment, the garden was silent, the children lost in thought. Then, as if on cue, they burst into excited chatter—fired up with more questions, more curiosity, and more love for their wise **Great-Grandpa**.

With a confident stride, **Ibrahim** stepped forward, his eyes filled with curiosity and determination. He respectfully sought permission, his voice carrying both eagerness and sincerity.

"**Great-Grandpa**, ***there are questions that have been lingering in my mind for a long time, questions that I believe only you can truly answer. Your wisdom, your vast experience, and the depth of your knowledge—shaped by years of study and reflection—make you the perfect guide in this journey of understanding. Today, I seek not just answers, but insights that will help me navigate the deeper meanings of life. May I go ahead?"***

Great-Grandpa smiled warmly, his eyes twinkling with anticipation. He gave a firm nod and raised his hand with a cheerful thumbs-up, signaling his approval. "Go ahead, my dear **Ibrahim**," he said with a chuckle. "I'm ready for your questions—let's see if I can match your curiosity with wisdom!"

Ibrahim *sat upright, his eyes filled with a mix of curiosity and determination.* ***"Great-Grandpa, my questions are deep, and I need your wisdom. Please answer them one by one, using both common sense and the insights of different faiths—Islam, Christianity, Judaism, Hinduism, Buddhism, and Sikhism."***

Great-Grandpa leaned back in his favorite armchair, stroking his beard thoughtfully. With a warm smile, he nodded. "Ah, **Ibrahim**, these are questions that have puzzled and enlightened humankind for centuries. Let's explore them together."

1. How do we discover our unique purpose in life?

Great-Grandpa took a deep sip of his coffee, then spoke with a steady, thoughtful tone.

"Discovering one's purpose is not about finding a single answer—it's a journey of self-discovery, growth, and connection."

- **Islam** teaches that human purpose is to worship and serve God, live righteously, and contribute to society. The Quran states: *"I did not create jinn and mankind except to worship Me."* (Quran 51:56) Worship, in Islam, includes kindness, honesty, and fulfilling one's role in society.
- **Christianity** teaches that purpose is found in love, faith, and service. Jesus said, *"Love the Lord your God with all your heart and love your neighbor as yourself."* (Mark 12:30-31)
- **Judaism** believes in *Tikkun Olam*, meaning "repairing the world." Life's purpose is to make the world a better place through righteous actions.
- **Hinduism** speaks of *Dharma*, one's duty based on their role in society. A person's purpose unfolds through responsibilities, moral actions, and devotion.
- **Buddhism** teaches that purpose is found in seeking enlightenment and reducing suffering through mindfulness and compassion.
- **Sikhism** emphasizes *Seva* (selfless service) and living a truthful life while remembering God.

"Purpose is not just about what we do, but how we live—with integrity, kindness, and faith."

2. Does one's purpose change over time?

Great-Grandpa chuckled. "Ah, Ibrahim, that is the beauty of life. Purpose is not fixed—it evolves as we grow."

- **Islam** teaches that life's purpose adapts to different stages. In youth, learning and self-improvement may be a focus, while later, guiding others becomes essential.
- **Christianity** encourages personal transformation, as seen in Paul's journey from persecutor to preacher.
- **Judaism** believes in lifelong learning. A young student may find purpose in studying, while an elder may find it in teaching.
- **Hinduism** divides life into *ashramas*—stages of life, including learning, family life, retirement, and spiritual liberation.
- **Buddhism** teaches that self-awareness and mindfulness help one adapt to new purposes as life changes.
- **Sikhism** sees purpose as dynamic—living truthfully, serving others, and remembering God, no matter the stage of life.

"Purpose is not a destination but a journey—one that shifts with time, wisdom, and experience."

3. What role do personal growth and self-awareness play in fulfilling life's purpose?

Great-Grandpa tapped his temple with a knowing smile.

"A person who does not understand themselves cannot understand their purpose."

- **Islam** teaches *Tazkiyah* (self-purification), encouraging reflection and self-improvement to fulfill one's purpose.
- **Christianity** emphasizes self-awareness through prayer and seeking God's guidance.
- **Judaism** encourages self-examination, especially during Yom Kippur, to align one's actions with righteousness.
- **Hinduism** promotes self-realization through meditation and devotion.
- **Buddhism** stresses mindfulness—awareness of thoughts and actions leads to wisdom and purpose.

- **Sikhism** teaches that true purpose is realized through honest living and constant remembrance of God.

"Growth and self-awareness are like a lamp—without them, the path to purpose remains in darkness."

4. Is helping others an essential part of life's purpose?

Great-Grandpa's face lit up. "Absolutely! Life is not just about personal success but about uplifting others."

- **Islam** strongly emphasizes charity (*Zakat*), with the Quran stating: *"Those who give in charity, their reward is with their Lord."* (Quran 2:274)
- **Christianity** teaches love and service. Jesus washed his disciples' feet to show humility in serving others.
- **Judaism** believes in *Tzedakah* (charity), which is a duty, not just an option.
- **Hinduism** encourages *Seva* (selfless service) as a spiritual duty.
- **Buddhism** teaches *Metta* (loving-kindness) and helping others as a path to enlightenment.
- **Sikhism** promotes *Langar* (free meals) as a symbol of serving humanity.

"The purpose of life is not in what we gain, but in what we give."

5. How do acts of kindness and compassion shape our purpose?

Great-Grandpa's voice softened. **"Kindness is not just an act—it is the foundation of a meaningful life."**

- **Islam** calls kindness an act of faith, as Prophet Muhammad (PBUH) said, "Even a smile is charity."

- **Christianity** teaches, "Do unto others as you would have them do unto you." (Luke 6:31)
- **Judaism** sees kindness as part of Chesed (loving-kindness), a pillar of faith.
- **Hinduism** believes in Ahimsa (non-violence and compassion) toward all beings.
- **Buddhism** teaches Karuna (compassion), which leads to a life free from suffering.
- **Sikhism** encourages daily acts of kindness and helping the less fortunate.

"Kindness is a ripple—small acts create waves that shape the world."

6. Why do religious teachings emphasize selflessness and charity?

Great-Grandpa exhaled deeply. **"Because, my dear Ibrahim, the soul is not nourished by wealth, but by giving."**

- **Islam** makes charity a duty, as wealth is seen as a trust from God.
- **Christianity** teaches that the greatest love is sacrificing for others.
- **Judaism** believes helping others brings one closer to God.
- **Hinduism** teaches *Karma Yoga*—selfless service leads to liberation.
- **Buddhism** views generosity as a way to eliminate attachment and ego.
- **Sikhism** sees service (*Seva*) as the highest form of worship.

"A life lived only for oneself is a life half-lived. True purpose is found in serving others."

Ibrahim sat back, absorbing the wisdom. **"Great-Grandpa,** this was the most enlightening conversation I have ever had!"

Great-Grandpa smiled, his heart full. "My dear **Ibrahim**, life's purpose is not a secret—it is written in our hearts. The key is to listen, learn, and live with faith, kindness, and wisdom."

The Essence of Life's Purpose

The garden stood still, the only sound being the gentle rustling of leaves, as if nature itself had paused to absorb the wisdom shared. The golden morning light bathed the scene, casting a warm glow on the thoughtful faces of **Ibrahim, Yousuf and Maryam**. Their eyes, once filled with excitement, now reflected deep contemplation as they processed the profound words of their **Great-Grandpa.**

Sensing the weight of the moment, **Great-Grandpa** leaned forward, his voice steady yet full of warmth. With a gentle smile, he said,

"My dear children, the essence of life's purpose is not found in wealth, status, or fleeting pleasures. It is discovered in the depth of our hearts, in the kindness we extend, in the wisdom we seek, and in the love we share. Every faith, every philosophy, in its own way, reminds us that life's true fulfillment comes from giving rather than taking, from serving rather than demanding, from understanding rather than judging.

Your purpose is not something you stumble upon—it is something you create, shape, and nurture. It evolves with time, as you learn, grow, and experience the world. Hold onto your faith, cultivate compassion, and seek knowledge, for these will guide you toward a life of meaning.

And remember, my dear ones, the greatest legacy is not what we leave behind in riches, but the impact we have on the lives of others."

A hush fell over the children, their hearts swelling with a newfound understanding. The breeze carried his words into the air, as if whispering them to the universe itself. **Yousuf**, the youngest, broke the silence with a soft yet determined voice, "**Great-Grandpa,** I will remember this forever."

Great-Grandpa chuckled, his eyes twinkling. "Then, my dear **Yousuf,** today's session was truly worth it."

And with that, the sun climbed higher, the garden once again alive with the rustling of leaves, the chirping of birds, and the quiet but profound realization that a new journey of purpose had just begun.

As the conversation deepened, the last but certainly not the least, **Maryam** stepped forward. Her eyes gleamed with curiosity, and her voice carried a certain weight—a mix of determination and contemplation. **She** had been listening keenly to **Yousuf** and **Ibrahim's** exchange with their **Great Grandpa,** absorbing every word, but now it was her turn.

Maryam: ***"Great Grandpa, my questions are different. They are not just about learning or understanding but about something deeper—something that defines our very existence. They are about purpose. I feel that many people, including us, often struggle to understand the true meaning of life. We get lost in distractions, and sometimes, in that confusion, we forget why we are here. I want to clear these doubts, for myself and for everyone who listens to you. Please answer my questions one by one so we can grasp the wisdom behind them."***

She took a deep breath and then continued, her voice steady yet eager.

> ***"How can we stay committed to our purpose despite difficulties?"***
> ***"What if we feel lost and don't know our purpose?"***
> ***"How do we balance personal ambitions with a greater purpose in life?"***
> ***"What has life taught you about purpose?"***
> ***"If you could give one piece of advice about finding purpose, what would it be?"***
> ***"How can the younger generation stay connected to a meaningful path?"***

Great Grandpa's smile deepened as he looked at **Maryam**. He could see the spark of wisdom in her eyes, the thirst for understanding something beyond just facts—something that gives direction to life itself. He took a deep breath and spoke in a calm yet profound tone.

1. How can we stay committed to our purpose despite difficulties?

"Maryam, commitment to purpose is like sailing a ship in the vast ocean. The waves will be rough, storms will come, and there will be times when the shore is nowhere in sight. But a sailor never abandons his ship just because the journey gets difficult. He adjusts his sails, steadies his hands on the wheel, and keeps moving forward. In life, challenges are inevitable. They test our patience, our faith, and our determination. But true commitment comes from resilience—when we remind ourselves why we started, and what lies ahead. Every difficulty you face is a lesson, shaping you into the person you are meant to be. If you hold on, the storm will pass, and the horizon will clear."

2. What if we feel lost and don't know our purpose?

Great Grandpa chuckled softly, his eyes twinkling with kindness.

"Ah, my dear, feeling lost is not a curse—it is a sign that you are searching. And searching is the first step towards finding. No one is born knowing their purpose. It unfolds like the pages of a book, one chapter at a time. When you feel lost, don't panic. Instead, pause. Observe. Ask yourself: What do I love? What makes me feel alive? What impact do I want to leave in this world? Sometimes, purpose is not found in big, grand moments, but in small, meaningful ones—the kindness you show, the people you inspire, the knowledge you seek. Keep searching, and your purpose will find you."

3. How do we balance personal ambitions with a greater purpose in life?

Great Grandpa leaned forward slightly, his voice filled with wisdom.

"Think of life as a tree. Your personal ambitions are like the branches—they reach out, they grow, they strive for sunlight. But the greater purpose is the roots—deep, strong, and unseen, giving life to everything above. A tree cannot stand without roots, and roots alone cannot bear fruit. If your personal ambitions are only for yourself, they will not sustain you. But if they are connected to a deeper purpose—one that benefits others, one that brings goodness to the world—then they will have meaning beyond just success. So, balance is not about choosing one over the other, but ensuring that your ambitions serve a purpose greater than yourself."

4. What has life taught you about purpose?

Great Grandpa's gaze softened as if he were looking back through the corridors of time.

"Life has taught me that purpose is not a destination—it is a journey. When I was young, I thought purpose meant achieving something great. But over time, I realized it is not about reaching a goal, but about how we walk the path. Purpose is found in moments—in the love we share, the people we uplift, the values we stand for. It is not measured by wealth or titles, but by the hearts we touch. And most importantly, life has taught me that purpose evolves. What may seem important today may change tomorrow, and that is the beauty of growth."

5. The Formula for a Meaningful and Purposeful Life

Maryam: ***"Great Grandpa, many people feel lost because they don't know their purpose in life. How can we discover it?"***

Great Grandpa: "Your purpose is not something you find—it is something you create. Serve others, follow your passion, and live with integrity."

Maryam: ***"If you could give us one golden rule for a good life, what would it be?"***

Great Grandpa: "Live in such a way that when you look back, you have no regrets."

Maryam: ***"What are the biggest mistakes people make that take them away from happiness?"***

Great Grandpa: "Chasing the wrong things—money over peace, pride over love, greed over gratitude."

Maryam: ***If you could give one piece of advice about finding purpose, what would it be?***

Great Grandpa's voice carried the weight of a lifetime as he spoke this time.

"Do not chase a purpose like a prize to be won. Live with sincerity, with curiosity, with kindness. Do what brings goodness to the world, and purpose will reveal itself in the most unexpected ways. Remember, purpose is not just about 'what' you do—it is about 'why' you do it. And if your 'why' is rooted in truth, then no matter where life takes you, you will always be on the right path."

6. How can the younger generation stay connected to a meaningful path?

Great Grandpa's face lit up with hope as he looked at **Maryam, Yousuf**, and **Ibrahim**.

"You, my dear children, are living in a world full of distractions. Technology, social media, endless streams of information—these things can either guide you or mislead you. The key is to stay grounded. Stay close to the values that make you a good human being. Surround yourself with people who inspire you, who remind you of the things that truly matter. Read, learn, ask questions, but most importantly—listen to your heart. A meaningful path is not found in the noise of the world, but in the quiet moments when you reflect on who you are and who you want to become. Keep your faith strong, your mind open, and your intentions pure, and you will never lose your way."

As **Great Grandpa** finished, there was silence. Not the silence of emptiness, but the silence of deep thought. **Maryam, Yousuf, and Ibrahim** looked at one another, as if something within them had shifted, as if they had found answers not just in words, but in the wisdom behind them.

Maryam, with a gentle smile, nodded. *"Thank you,* ***Great Grandpa.*** *You have not just answered my questions—you have given us a compass to navigate life."*

Great Grandpa chuckled softly, his heart full. *"Ah, my dear, the compass was always within you. I just helped you see it."*

By this time, the golden sun had begun its slow descent, casting long shadows across the veranda. A gentle evening breeze rustled through the trees, carrying with it a sense of contentment and quiet reflection. Yet, amidst the depth of their conversation, exhaustion had crept in—not just for the children but even for **Great Grandpa**, whose wisdom had poured forth like an endless river.

Just then, a familiar voice called from inside.

"Lunch is ready!" **GrandMa's** warm yet firm tone echoed through the house, signaling that it was time to set aside deep thoughts and nourish their bodies.

Great Grandpa stretched his arms with a knowing smile. "Ah, my dear **Maryam, Yousuf, and Ibrahim,** wisdom may feed the soul, but nothing feeds an empty stomach like GrandMa's cooking. Let's pause our session here and continue another day."

The children exchanged glances, a mix of satisfaction and lingering curiosity in their eyes. But as the delicious aroma from the dining area reached them, the excitement of food quickly replaced their philosophical musings.

As they got up, **Great Grandpa** added with a twinkle in his eye, *"And don't forget—after a good meal and some rest, we have an important event at 4:00 PM. The table tennis tournament! Remember, the winner gets a surprise reward from me."*

That last announcement sent a jolt of energy through the tired faces. **Yousuf and Ibrahim** immediately started discussing strategies, while **Maryam**, though more thoughtful, couldn't hide her competitive spirit.

With laughter and light chatter filling the air, they all made their way inside, carrying with them the warmth of wisdom, the joy of family, and the excitement of the challenge ahead.

Little did they know, the lessons of purpose and determination they had just learned would soon be tested—not in words, but in action.

Session Eight

Timeless Talks: Great-Grandfather's Conversations with Curious Minds

Understanding Diseases and Their Impact on Life

The golden morning unfolds with a quiet charm, as beams of soft sunlight dance through the family room windows, casting warm patterns on the floor. Outside, a gentle breeze rustles the leaves, carrying the fresh scent of dew-kissed grass and the distant chirping of birds. It is the perfect start to yet another cherished weekend—one that brings not just the promise of a new day but also the joy of tradition.

Great-Grandpa, a man of discipline and grace, has already begun his day. After his dawn prayers, he steps out for his morning walk, an essential part of his routine. Dressed in his signature attire—simple yet dignified—he moves at a steady pace, his trusted walking stick tapping rhythmically against the ground. With every step, he breathes in the crisp air, greeting familiar sights along the way—the blooming flowers, the fluttering butterflies, the gentle hum of the waking world. His presence carries an aura of wisdom, a quiet strength that speaks of a life well-lived.

Returning home, he engages in another beloved ritual—brewing his own black coffee. The rich aroma swirls through the air, blending with the warmth of the morning. Settling into his favorite armchair, he takes a slow, thoughtful sip, savoring the stillness before the delightful storm of laughter and chatter that is about to descend upon him.

And then, like clockwork, it begins. From upstairs, the unmistakable sound of tiny voices fills the house—giggling, singing, and the playful chatter of his beloved **great-grandchildren.** Their excitement is palpable as they prepare for their treasured weekend ritual—"**Conversations with Great-**

Grandpa." The wooden stairs creak under their hurried footsteps as they rush down, their voices growing louder, brimming with enthusiasm.

The moment they reach him, their faces light up with joy as they sing in chorus, "GOOD MORNING, GREAT-GRANDPA!" Their laughter rings through the room, a melody sweeter than any morning bird's song.

Great-Grandpa, his heart swelling with love, smiles warmly and responds in his deep, affectionate voice, "A VERY GOOD MORNING, MY DEAREST KIDS!" Opening his arms wide, he welcomes them into a warm embrace. It is a moment of pure love, a connection beyond words—a bridge between generations built on affection, wisdom, and an unbreakable bond.

With playful curiosity, he asks, "So, how was your night? Did you sleep well?"

They exchange glances and giggle, their eyes twinkling with mischief. "Yes, **Great-Grandpa**, we slept well, but we had so many dreams about ghosts! It was scary!"

Great-Grandpa chuckles, gently patting their heads. "Ah, those mischievous dreams! But remember, dreams are just stories your mind tells you. And with a brave heart, no ghost can ever frighten you!"

Moving on, he inquires, "Did you have your breakfast?"

Their faces brighten as they eagerly reply, "Yes, **Great-Grandpa**! Today's breakfast was delicious—chocolate-flavored cornflakes, boiled eggs, a banana, and an apple!"

Nodding approvingly, he smiles. "That sounds wonderful! A strong start to the day." Then, raising an eyebrow playfully, he asks, "And what about your glass of fresh orange juice?"

A slight pause, followed by cheeky grins. "No, not yet, **Great-Grandpa**. We'll have it during the break in our conversation!"

He chuckles at their clever response. "Ah, a smart idea indeed! Alright then, let's begin our wonderful morning together."

And so, with hearts full of love and minds eager for stories, another magical session of wisdom, laughter, and boundless imagination begins—a morning ritual that will be etched in their memories forever.

As **Great-Grandpa** glanced around the lively gathering, his sharp eyes suddenly noticed something amiss. A familiar little face was missing from the crowd. With a gentle yet concerned voice, he asked, "Wait a minute, my dear ones... where is my darling **Lucy**? Why didn't you bring her along?"

The children exchanged quick glances before **Maryam** spoke up, "**Great-Grandpa**, **Lucy** wasn't feeling well this morning. She's still sleeping. But as soon as she wakes up, Grandma will give her breakfast and send her to join us."

A slight look of concern crossed **Great-Grandpa**'s face, but before he could respond—"Mao Mao!"

A familiar, playful sound echoed through the room. The children turned toward the staircase, and there she was—**Lucy**, rubbing her sleepy eyes yet beaming with excitement! She had woken up and, without wasting a moment, rushed downstairs to be with everyone.

Shaking hands mischievously with **Maryam**, **Ibrahim**, and **Yousuf**, **Lucy** wasted no time before leaping straight into **Great-Grandpa**'s lap. He let out a hearty laugh, his arms embracing her with warmth and love. "Ah, my little **Lucy**! So, you couldn't stay away from us, could you?"

The entire room burst into applause as the children clapped in delight, celebrating Lucy's surprise arrival. The joy on their faces was undeniable—what was once incomplete was now whole again.

Great-Grandpa, his heart full, looked around at his beloved **great-grandchildren** and smiled. "Now the group is complete! And with that, we are ready to move forward with our session."

With excitement buzzing in the air, the conversation was about to begin—another memorable gathering where love, wisdom, and shared moments would create yet another cherished chapter in their family's story.

As the joyful echoes of laughter begin to settle, a sense of eager anticipation fills the room. The **great-grandchildren**, now comfortably seated around **Great-Grandpa**, exchange glances, their curious minds brimming with questions.

Maryam, the ever-confident and thoughtful one, steps forward with a bright, determined expression. With a respectful nod, she declares, "Today, our topic of conversation is '**Understanding Diseases and Their Impact on Life**.'" Her voice carries a mix of enthusiasm and seriousness, reflecting the importance of the subject.

She pauses for a moment before continuing, "**Great-Grandpa**, may we begin today's questionnaire?" Her eyes shine with the excitement of leading the discussion, knowing that this will be yet another enriching conversation filled with wisdom and discovery.

Great-Grandpa, leaning slightly forward in his favorite armchair, clasps his hands together and smiles warmly. He nods approvingly, his gaze filled with admiration. "What a thoughtful and relevant topic, my dear **Maryam**! I truly appreciate your selection. Understanding diseases—especially the new and emerging ones—is indeed a necessity in today's world. Modern society is struggling to combat these challenges, and knowledge is our strongest weapon."

He takes a thoughtful sip of his black coffee before setting the cup down, his expression turning more serious yet gentle. "Diseases not only affect individuals but also shape families, communities, and even entire nations. Learning about them, their causes, and how to prevent them is an essential step toward a healthier future. I am more than happy to discuss this with you all."

With a slight gesture of his hand, he encourages **Maryam, Ibrahim and Yousuf**. "Go ahead, my dear. Let's begin this important discussion."

Excitement sparks in the children's eyes as they lean forward, ready to dive into another enlightening session—one that will not only deepen their understanding of the world but also strengthen the bond they share with their beloved **Great-Grandpa**.

Why do people get sick?

Maryam: ***Great Grandpa, why do people get sick?***
Great Grandpa: We get sick due to germs, weak immunity, poor lifestyle, or environmental factors. Viruses and bacteria spread through air, water, and touch. A weak immune system makes us prone to infections. Unhealthy food, lack of exercise, and stress weaken our body. Pollution and weather changes also trigger diseases. Genetics can pass illnesses from parents to children. Aging makes the body weaker and more vulnerable. Good hygiene, a balanced diet, and exercise help prevent sickness. Proper rest and stress management strengthen immunity. Staying healthy requires a strong body and mindful habits.

What should we do to stay healthy?

Maryam: ***What should we do to stay healthy?***
Great Grandpa: Eat healthy food, drink lots of water, wash your hands, play outside, and get enough sleep. These are like superpowers that help your body stay strong!

Why do some diseases spread from one person to another?

Ibrahim: Great Grandpa, *why do some diseases spread from one person to another?*
Great Grandpa: Some diseases are caused by viruses and bacteria that travel through air, water, or touch. When an infected person sneezes or coughs, tiny germs spread and can make others sick. That's why washing hands and covering our mouth when we cough is important.

Why do some diseases last a long time while others go away quickly?

Ibrahim: *Why do some diseases last a long time while others go away quickly?*
Great Grandpa: Some diseases go away quickly, while others last long due to their nature and our immune system. Acute diseases (like colds or flu) heal fast, while chronic diseases (like diabetes or arthritis) persist for years. Stronger germs, weak immunity, or lack of proper care can prolong illness. Healthy habits and treatment help recovery.

How do diseases change people's lives?

Yousuf: **Great Grandpa**, ***how do diseases change people's lives?***
Great Grandpa: Diseases affect daily life, causing pain, stress, and limitations. **Chronic illnesses** (like diabetes or arthritis) require lifelong care, changing diet, work, and routine. **Severe infections** may lead to long recovery times and weakness. Mental health can suffer due to stress and anxiety. Medical costs and frequent hospital visits add financial strain. Support from family and a healthy lifestyle help manage the impact.

Can we stop diseases before they happen?

Yousuf: ***Can we stop diseases before they happen?***
Great Grandpa: Yes, many diseases can be prevented with healthy habits. Good hygiene (handwashing, clean food, safe water) stops infections. A strong immune system (healthy diet, exercise, enough sleep) fights off illnesses. Vaccinations protect against serious diseases. Regular checkups help detect issues early. Avoiding smoking, alcohol, and stress lowers health risks. Prevention is better than cure!

"The growing burden of serious diseases—heart conditions, diabetes, cancer, and mysterious new epidemics—reminds us how fragile life truly is."?

Maryam: ***"Great Grandpa, today we hear about so many serious diseases—heart problems, diabetes, cancer, and even new epidemics. Were these illnesses common in your time?"***

Great Grandpa: "Not as common as they are today, my dear. Many diseases have increased because of changes in lifestyle, diet, pollution, and stress. In my younger days, people led simpler lives, ate fresh food, and walked more. That made a big difference."

Yousuf: ***"Is it true that stress can cause diseases like heart problems and high blood pressure?"***

Great Grandpa: "Absolutely! Stress is like a silent poison—it weakens the body from within. Worrying too much about things beyond your control harms both the heart and the mind."

Ibrahim: ***"Diabetes is becoming very common, even in young people. What causes it, and how can we prevent it?"***

Great Grandpa: Diabetes is rising, even in young people, due to unhealthy diets, lack of exercise, obesity, genetics, and stress. Type 1 diabetes is genetic, while Type 2 is mostly lifestyle-related. Prevention includes healthy eating, regular exercise, maintaining a healthy weight, managing stress, and avoiding sugary foods. Regular checkups help early detection and control.

"Cancer rates keep climbing—what's fueling this relentless spread?"

Maryam: ***"What about cancer? It seems to be spreading more than ever. Why is that happening?"***

Great Grandpa: Cancer is increasing due to unhealthy lifestyles, pollution, processed foods, smoking, alcohol, and rising stress levels. Genetics and aging also raise the risk. Environmental factors like radiation, chemicals, and air pollution contribute to its spread. Modern diets, with preservatives and additives, may also play a role. Early detection through regular checkups and a healthy lifestyle can help prevent and manage cancer.

Maryam: Dear **Great-Grandpa,** ***I have a dream—I want to become a doctor, but not just any doctor. I want to dedicate my life to the field of oncology and make a name for myself as a distinguished cancer specialist. I understand that cancer is a deadly disease, its treatment is often painful, expensive, and not always successful. Despite great advancements, we still need more research to make cancer treatment as effective and accessible as TB or other chronic diseases, which were once fatal but are now easily treatable.***

Could you guide me on how I can achieve this goal? Also, please pray for my success, my dear **Great-Grandpa.**

Great Grandpa: My dearest **Maryam**, nothing makes me prouder than to hear you speak with such passion and purpose about your future! Your dream is noble, and your commitment to alleviating human suffering is truly commendable. Becoming a distinguished oncologist will not only require intelligence and hard work but also deep compassion and perseverance.

Let me give you some guidance on your journey:

1. A Strong Educational Foundation

To become an oncologist, you must first pursue excellence in science. Pay special attention to Biology, Chemistry, and Physics in school. Develop a deep understanding of how the human body functions, how diseases like cancer develop, and how medical treatments work.

2. The Path to Medical School

After school, you will need to:

- Earn a medical degree (MBBS or MD) from a reputable institution.
- Specialize in oncology by choosing the right postgraduate program (MD in Oncology or DM in Medical Oncology).
- Keep up with cutting-edge research because medicine, especially oncology, is evolving every day.

3. The Power of Research and Innovation

You have rightly said that cancer treatment needs more breakthroughs. The good news is that scientists worldwide are working on immunotherapy, targeted therapy, and gene therapy to make treatments more effective and affordable. As a future oncologist, you can contribute to research and clinical trials that may one day lead to a permanent cure.

4. Compassion and Communication – The True Strength of a Doctor

Beyond knowledge and skill, an oncologist needs an extraordinary heart. Cancer patients and their families go through immense emotional pain. A great doctor doesn't just treat the disease—he or she heals the person with kindness, encouragement, and hope.

5. Challenges and Strength

Your journey will be tough—long hours of study, years of training, and heartbreaking moments with patients. But remember, every patient you save, every family you comfort, and every life you improve will be a testament to your dedication.

6. The Role of Faith and Prayers

Maryam, I will not only pray for your success but also remind you that when you work with sincerity and a pure heart, your prayers turn into reality. Trust in your abilities, believe in the power of knowledge, and always seek blessings from your elders and Allah (God).

You can achieve greatness, my child. Keep your eyes on the goal, never give up, and remember that your **Great-Grandpa** will always be proud of you!

Maryam: Oh, **Great-Grandpa,** your words have filled my heart with hope and determination! I will follow this path with all my energy, and one day, I promise, I will make you proud as **Dr. Maryam**, **the oncologist who brought hope to thousands!**

Yousuf: ***"Are modern medicines helping, or is traditional healing better?"***

Great Grandpa: Both modern medicine and traditional healing have their benefits. Modern medicine uses advanced research, surgeries, and drugs to treat diseases quickly and effectively, especially for infections, cancer, and emergencies. Traditional healing (herbal remedies, Ayurveda, acupuncture) focuses on natural treatments, long-term wellness, and fewer side effects. Combining both—modern science for critical care and traditional methods for prevention and overall health—offers the best approach.

The Rise of Epidemics and Global Health Concerns

Maryam: "**Great-Grandpa,** ***we hear about new diseases and epidemics spreading worldwide. Why do you think this is happening so frequently now?"***

Great Grandpa: Ah, **Maryam**, that's an important question. Epidemics and new diseases have always existed, but they seem to be increasing now due to several reasons:

1. Globalization & Travel – In the past, diseases remained confined to one region. Now, with people traveling across the world in hours, infections spread faster than ever.
2. Deforestation & Wildlife Encroachment – When humans destroy forests, they come into contact with new viruses from animals that were once isolated. Many deadly diseases originated this way.
3. Climate Change – Rising temperatures, floods, and changing weather patterns create new environments for viruses and bacteria to thrive.
4. Overuse of Antibiotics & Weak Immunity – Many people rely on medicines unnecessarily, leading to antibiotic resistance, where bacteria become stronger and harder to treat.
5. Poor Lifestyle Choices – Processed foods, lack of exercise, and stress weaken immunity, making people more vulnerable to infections.

Diseases spread faster because the world is more connected than before. The key to protection is strong immunity, good hygiene, and responsible medical care.

Ibrahim: "Great-Grandpa, ***some epidemics like COVID-19 changed the world completely. How do you think societies should prepare for future pandemics?"***

Great Grandpa: Ibrahim, pandemics are like unexpected storms—they come suddenly and test our strength. The lesson from COVID-19 is that we must always be prepared. Here's how:

1. Invest in Healthcare – Governments must strengthen hospitals, medical research, and vaccine production. A strong healthcare system can save millions of lives.
2. Promote Preventive Care – Instead of only treating diseases, societies must focus on prevention through vaccinations, hygiene, and public awareness.
3. Encourage Local Production of Medicine & Supplies – During pandemics, global supply chains break down. Countries must ensure they can produce essential medicines, masks, and medical equipment locally.
4. Build a Culture of Preparedness – People must be educated about how to respond to outbreaks without panic. Simple steps like social distancing, hygiene, and wearing masks saved lives during COVID-19.
5. Strengthen Community Bonds – During crises, people need support. Family, neighbors, and communities must help each other rather than isolating in fear.

The world has seen pandemics before, and it will see them again. But with knowledge and unity, we can always fight back.

Mental and Emotional Health in a Fast-Paced World

Yousuf: "Great-Grandpa, *why do people today seem more stressed and anxious, even though life has become easier with technology?"*
Great Grandpa: Ah, **Yousuf**, that is a deep question. Life has indeed become easier in many ways—machines do our work, communication is instant, and medical advancements have made life longer. But with these advancements, we have also lost balance in our lives.

Here's why stress and anxiety have increased:

1. **Constant Competition** – The modern world is always pushing people to achieve more—higher grades, better jobs, more money. This endless race creates pressure and mental exhaustion.
2. **Too Much Screen Time** – People spend hours on phones, social media, and TV. Instead of real human interaction, they compare their lives to fake, filtered images online, which leads to dissatisfaction.
3. **Less Family Time** – In the past, families ate meals together, shared stories, and supported each other. Today, everyone is busy with their own schedules, leading to loneliness.
4. **Lack of Spiritual & Inner Peace** – People chase material success but neglect their inner well-being. Prayer, meditation, and simple reflection bring peace, but these habits are disappearing.
5. **Poor Sleep & Unhealthy Lifestyles** – Irregular sleep, junk food, and lack of exercise affect mental health. A tired body leads to a tired mind.

The key to good mental health is balance—work hard, but also rest. Use technology, but don't let it control you. Earn money, but don't forget the real wealth of family, health, and faith.

Yousuf: Great Grandpa, *does that mean as time goes on, if we fail to control stress and anxiety and don't improve our lifestyle, our lifespan will continue to shrink? Are we unknowingly shortening our own lives?*

Great Grandpa: That's a very insightful question, **Yousuf!** You are absolutely right to think about the impact of stress and lifestyle on lifespan. While genetics play a role in how long we live, our daily choices, habits, and mental well-being significantly influence our overall health and longevity.

Here's a logical way to look at it:

1. **The Silent Killer** – Stress: Chronic stress triggers the release of hormones like cortisol, which, in excess, can weaken the immune system, increase blood pressure, and accelerate aging. If we don't learn to manage stress, it slowly eats away at our physical and mental health, reducing our lifespan.

2. **Modern Lifestyle vs. Natural Living**: Our ancestors lived simpler lives, closer to nature, with healthier diets, physical activity, and strong community bonds. Today, excessive screen time, poor eating habits, lack of sleep, and social isolation have introduced new health risks that didn't exist before.

3. **Mind-Body Connection**: Anxiety and stress aren't just emotions—they physically affect the heart, brain, and immune system. A constantly anxious mind can lead to diseases like heart attacks, strokes, and even certain types of cancer. Scientists have found that happier people with positive mindsets tend to live longer and healthier lives.

4. **Shrinking Lifespan Trend**: Over centuries, medical advancements have increased life expectancy, but in some regions, we now see it declining again due to poor lifestyle choices, stress, and mental health issues. This means that if we don't take action, we could be reversing the progress humanity has made.

The good news, **Yousuf,** is that we are not powerless! By practicing mindfulness, staying active, eating nutritious food, sleeping well, and maintaining strong social and family connections, we can extend both the quality and length of our lives.

So, remember—our lifespan isn't just determined by fate; it is shaped by how we choose to live each day. Wouldn't it be wise to take control before time slips away?

Maryam: "Great-Grandpa, *how can we improve our emotional well-being in such a fast-paced world?"*

Great Grandpa: Maryam, emotional well-being is like a garden—you must nurture it daily to keep it healthy. Here's how:

1. **Limit Social Media & Technology Use** – Spend less time on screens and more time with real people. Talk to family, play outside, and enjoy nature.
2. **Develop a Routine** – Sleeping and waking up on time, eating healthy, and exercising regularly keep both body and mind strong.
3. **Practice Gratitude** – Every day, remind yourself of the blessings you have. A grateful heart is a happy heart.
4. **Talk About Your Feelings** – Don't bottle up emotions. Share your worries with loved ones. Talking heals.
5. **Help Others** – Acts of kindness bring inner peace. Helping someone in need, even with a small gesture, strengthens the soul.
6. **Find Time for Spirituality & Reflection** – Pray, meditate, or simply sit in silence. The world moves fast, but your heart needs moments of stillness.

Happiness doesn't come from having everything—it comes from being content with what you have. When you learn this, no matter how fast the world moves, you will always remain at peace.

Remember, children, life is not a race—it's a journey. Walk it wisely, and you will always find peace.

Maryam: *"Physical health is important, but what about mental health? Depression and anxiety are increasing everywhere. Why is that?"*

Great Grandpa: "Because people have forgotten how to live in the present. They either worry about the future or regret the past. A restless mind leads to a restless body."

Maryam: Great Grandpa: ***Have you ever wondered how nature holds the power to heal our worries, cure diseases, lift our spirits, and wash away the burdens of life? How does the natural world soothe our minds, energize our bodies, and bring peace to our hearts?***

Absolutely! Nature has an incredible ability to heal and uplift the human mind and body. Here's how nature helps in different aspects of life:

1. Physical Healing:

- Fresh Air: Breathing in fresh air improves lung function and overall oxygen levels in the body.
- Sunlight: Exposure to sunlight helps produce Vitamin D, which strengthens bones and boosts immunity.
- Medicinal Plants: Many natural herbs, like turmeric, ginger, and neem, have healing properties that prevent and cure diseases.

2. Mental and Emotional Healing:

- Stress Reduction: Spending time in green spaces lowers cortisol levels, reducing stress and anxiety.
- Improved Mood: Being in nature releases endorphins and serotonin, which help combat depression.
- Better Sleep: Natural environments regulate sleep cycles, leading to deeper and more restful sleep.

3. Spiritual and Psychological Benefits:

- Peace and Mindfulness: The sounds of birds, flowing water, and rustling leaves create a calming effect, helping in meditation and mindfulness.

- Connection with Life: Observing nature teaches patience, resilience, and the beauty of life's cycles.
- Sense of Purpose: Gardening, hiking, or simply walking in nature fosters a sense of fulfillment and gratitude.

4. Cognitive and Social Benefits:

- Boosts Creativity: Exposure to nature stimulates creative thinking and problem-solving skills.
- Enhances Focus: Natural surroundings improve attention spans and memory retention.
- Promotes Social Bonding: Outdoor activities bring families and communities closer together.

Nature is truly a gift to humanity, offering countless benefits that heal the body, mind, and soul. Do you have any favorite ways to connect with nature?

Ibrahim: ***"How can we take care of our mental health?"***

Great Grandpa: "By simplifying life. Limit screen time, spend time in nature, and talk to people instead of living through social media. Find peace in faith, family, and meaningful work."

Ancient Longevity and Healing: A Great-Grandfather's Wisdom

Yousuf: Great-Grandpa, ***I read somewhere that people in ancient times lived much longer than today. Some even lived for hundreds of years! Is that true?***

Great-Grandpa: Ah, my dear **Yousuf,** what a fascinating topic you've brought up! Throughout history, ancient scriptures and religious texts have spoken of extraordinary lifespans—far beyond what we see today.

Take, for example, the stories of the prophets and sages across different traditions. In the Bible and the Quran, Prophet Noah is said to have lived for **950 years**, guiding generations before the Great Flood. Similarly, Hindu scriptures speak of revered sages and deities who lived for centuries, possessing wisdom that spanned ages.

Now, one might wonder—were humans really capable of living for such long periods, or is there a deeper meaning behind these accounts? Some scholars believe these lifespans symbolized **wisdom and legacy**, while others argue that ancient environmental conditions, diets, and simpler lifestyles may have contributed to longer lives.

But here's the key thought, my dear—while our physical years may be shorter today, the **impact we leave behind** can stretch far beyond our lifetime. What truly matters is not just how long we live, but how meaningfully we spend our days. Would you rather live a long life filled with stress and regret or a shorter one full of wisdom, love, and purpose?

Yousuf: ***But how is that possible? Today, most people barely live beyond 80 or 90 years.***

Great-Grandpa: There are several theories. In early human civilization, the environment was purer—there was no pollution, no processed foods, and no industrial waste contaminating air, water, and land. People lived in harmony with nature, eating organic, natural foods, drinking fresh water from rivers and springs, and breathing unpolluted air.

Yousuf: ***So, their food and environment helped them live longer?***

Great-Grandpa: Yes, that's one reason. Another reason is genetics. Early humans were stronger, and their immune systems were more resilient because they had not yet been exposed to the many viruses, bacteria, and environmental hazards we face today. Also, they lived in small, isolated communities, reducing the spread of infectious diseases.

Maryam: ***But what about diseases? If there were no hospitals or modern medicine, how did they treat illnesses?***

Great-Grandpa: Excellent question! Ancient civilizations relied on natural remedies, herbal medicine, and traditional healing methods. For example:

- **Herbal Medicine**: People used plants, roots, and leaves to cure diseases. Ayurveda in India, Traditional Chinese Medicine, and Greek and Islamic medicine all relied on herbs like turmeric, ginger, honey, and black seeds.
- **Hijama (Cupping Therapy)**: This was practiced by the ancient Egyptians, Chinese, and Arabs to remove toxins from the body.
- **Spiritual and Faith Healing**: Many believed in the power of prayers, meditation, and divine blessings to cure illnesses.
- **Diet and Fasting**: Ancient civilizations emphasized healthy eating and fasting to cleanse the body and heal naturally.
- **Bone Setting & Surgery**: Some ancient healers were skilled in treating fractures, wounds, and infections using primitive surgical tools.

Ibrahim: ***That sounds amazing! But why don't we use these methods anymore?***

Great-Grandpa: Well, we still do in some ways. Many modern medicines are based on ancient herbal knowledge. But with the advancement of science, synthetic drugs, and hospitals, we have moved toward quicker solutions. However, many people are now returning to natural healing, realizing that modern medicine sometimes treats symptoms rather than the root cause.

Ibrahim: ***So, in a way, ancient people had a healthier lifestyle than us?***

Great-Grandpa: Precisely! Despite lacking modern medicine, they lived closer to nature, ate fresh food, avoided stress from modern life, and trusted their body's natural healing power. We can learn a lot from their way of living!

All three Children together: *That's interesting,* ***Great-Grandpa****! Maybe we should start eating like them and living a simpler life too!*

Great-Grandpa: A wise thought, my dear! A balance of ancient wisdom and modern science is the key to a long and healthy life.

Session Nine

"Threads of Time: A Dialogue Across Generations"

"Beyond Materialism: Unveiling Life's True Purpose"

The Pursuit of a Simple and Peaceful Life

The long-awaited weekend had finally arrived—a day **Great Grandpa** and his **great-grandchildren** cherished beyond words. It was their sacred time, where laughter intertwined with wisdom, where stories of the past met the dreams of the future, and where love flowed effortlessly like a river of golden light.

As usual, Great Grandpa, a disciplined ex-army officer, was up before dawn. After his early morning prayers, he stepped out for his brisk walk, feeling the crisp morning air kiss his face. The world around him was awakening, bathed in the soft glow of the first golden rays of the sun. A gentle breeze whispered through the trees, carrying with it the fresh scent of blooming flowers and damp earth. High above, white clouds drifted lazily, as if dancing to an unheard melody. The distant chirping of birds created a soothing symphony, and for a brief moment, time seemed to pause in this breathtaking serenity.

Back in the family room, he settled into his favorite armchair, cradling a steaming mug of coffee in his hands. The warmth seeped into his fingers, much like the warmth of his memories—stories from a life well-lived, moments of triumph, loss, love, and adventure. As he gazed out the window, his thoughts wandered to his beloved **great-grandchildren**, the little sparks of joy who filled his heart with boundless happiness. How he longed for their giggles, their endless questions, and the sparkle in their eyes when they unraveled life's mysteries together.

And then, like the sweetest melody, muffled whispers and soft giggles floated down the hallway, growing clearer with every passing second. His heart swelled with anticipation—this was the moment he had been waiting for! The excited patter of tiny feet thundered down the stairs, a joyful rhythm that filled the house with life.

Bursting into the family room, their voices rang in unison, bright and full of love—

"Good morning, Great-Grandpa!"

Trailing behind the exuberant children was little **Lucy**, adorned with a vibrant garland of fresh flowers—a heartfelt surprise the great-grandchildren had meticulously prepared for their beloved **Great-Grandpa**. Her tail wagged furiously, and her eyes sparkled with excitement as she approached him. With a soft bark, Lucy greeted her greatest friend, anticipating the moment she would curl up in his cozy lap, lulled into slumber by the soothing cadence of his stories.

In various cultures, floral garlands symbolize love, respect, and celebration. By adorning **Lucy** with the garland, the **great-grandchildren** expressed their deep affection, creating a moment rich with universal symbolism and love.

This touching gesture exemplifies the profound connection between **great-grandparents** and **great-grandchildren**. Such relationships are invaluable, fostering mutual respect, love, and a deep sense of belonging. Great-Grandparents often serve as pillars of wisdom and stability, enriching their great-grandchildren's lives with stories, guidance, and unwavering support.

In this tender moment, the family wove a tapestry of love and shared joy, strengthening the bonds that connect them across generations.

Their tiny arms stretched wide as they ran toward him, their faces beaming with pure delight. With a loving smile, **Great-Grandpa** set his coffee mug aside and opened his arms, gathering them into a warm embrace. Their laughter, their energy, their boundless love wrapped around him like a soft, comforting blanket, filling every corner of his heart.

At that moment, nothing else in the world mattered. No worries, no passing time—just the joy of being together. **Great-Grandpa** and his beloved **great-grandchildren**, bound by love, wisdom, and a silent promise to cherish these fleeting moments forever.

Yousuf, Ibrahim, and Maryam gathered eagerly around **Great-Grandpa,** their eyes wide with curiosity and anticipation. These moments were treasured; what began as simple conversations often transformed into profound lessons that lingered in their young minds. Today was no exception. They had pressing questions about **money, materialism, and the true essence of a peaceful life.**

As they settled in, **Lucy,** their faithful canine companion, leaped gracefully into **Great-Grandpa's** lap, her tail wagging in contentment. Nestling into the crook of his arm, she exuded comfort and readiness, as if sensing the importance of the discussion about to unfold.

Great-Grandpa looked at each of them, his eyes twinkling with wisdom and warmth. **"My dear ones,"** he began, his voice gentle yet resonant, "money is a tool, not the treasure. It's essential to understand its value but not to be ensnared by it."

He shared stories from his youth, recalling how his grandparents lived modestly, working diligently and saving every penny they could. "They taught me that a penny earned is a penny saved," he said, echoing the timeless adage. "Their sacrifices weren't just for survival but to build a foundation for future generations."

The children listened intently as he spoke of the dangers of materialism. "We don't need everything we want," he continued, quoting his own grandmother. "True contentment comes from appreciating what we have, not from chasing what we don't."

Lucy nuzzled closer, her presence a soothing balm. **Great-Grandpa** smiled, gently stroking her fur. "Even **Lucy** understands," he chuckled. "She finds joy in the simplest things—a warm lap, a gentle touch. We, too, can learn from her simplicity."

He leaned in closer, his tone earnest. "Remember, investing in yourself and others brings true fulfillment. Share your blessings, help those in need, and you'll find that peace isn't bought—it's earned through love and kindness."

As the conversation flowed, the room seemed to glow with a special warmth. The children felt the weight of his words, understanding that the lessons imparted were gifts far more valuable than any material possession. They were equipped with wisdom to navigate life's complexities, guided by love, simplicity, and a generous spirit.

In that cozy room, surrounded by the gentle hum of shared stories and the soft presence of **Lucy**, **Great-Grandpa** and his **great-grandchildren** forged a bond that transcended generations—a testament to the enduring power of family, wisdom, and unconditional love.

At first glance, these seemed like topics far beyond their years, something only adults pondered over. But times had changed. Today's children were sharper, wiser, and more aware than ever before. Unlike a century ago, when such discussions were reserved for the elderly and scholars, young minds today grasped the weight of these subjects with surprising maturity.

Great Grandpa knew this wasn't going to be an easy discussion. Finance and materialism weren't just about numbers and possessions—they shaped the way people lived, influenced their happiness, and even decided the kind of world they would grow up in. He smiled to himself. This is no ordinary talk... This is a discussion that could win a **Nobel Prize** if explained the right way!

He took a deep breath, ready to embark on yet another fascinating journey of thoughts and ideas with his beloved **great-grandchildren.** How would they respond? How far could their young minds go? And, most importantly, how could he help them see beyond material wealth and truly understand what makes life rich and fulfilling?

One thing was certain—this was going to be a conversation to remember.

*After receiving the signal from **Great Grandpa, Maryam** confidently stepped forward to lead the discussion. She glanced at her brothers before turning to him with a serious expression.*

"The paradox of prosperity: when wealth grows, but happiness fades."

Maryam: "Great Grandpa, in today's world, everything seems to revolve around money. We are told that financial success is the key to happiness. But why do so many wealthy people still seem unhappy? Is money really the ultimate goal in life?"

Great Grandpa leaned back in his chair, smiling at **Maryam's** thoughtful question. He took a moment to sip his coffee before answering.

"That's an excellent question, Maryam," he began. "Money is a tool, not a destination. Imagine money as a car. A car helps you reach your destination, but it is not the journey itself. If you don't know where you're going, even the fastest car won't make you happy."

He glanced at their eager faces, a gentle smile playing on his lips, and continued, "Money can buy comfort, security, and even fleeting moments of happiness, but have you ever wondered why some of the wealthiest people still struggle with loneliness, stress, and even depression? It's because true happiness doesn't come with a price tag—it comes from the things money can never buy: love, kindness, inner peace, and a sense of purpose.

Einstein understood this well. He lived a life of simplicity, valuing knowledge over riches. He once said, 'Possessions, outward success, publicity, luxury—to me these have always been contemptible.' He knew that the greatest treasures in life aren't found in a bank account, but in the moments we share, the kindness we give, and the peace we carry within."

Yousuf, *always the logical thinker, leaned forward.* ***"But Great Grandpa, if money isn't everything, why do people work so hard to earn more and more of it?"***

Great Grandpa *chuckled.* "Because the world teaches us that success is measured in numbers—salary, bank balance, the size of your house, or the brand of your car. But do you know the wealthiest people in history, the ones truly remembered, were not those with the most money, but those who gave the most to the world? Look at people like **Prophet Muhammad** (PBUH), **Mother Teresa**, **Mahatma Gandhi, Nelson Mandela, George Washington** or even **great scientists and teachers.** They focused on something far greater than money—they sought knowledge, wisdom, and the betterment of others. And that's why their names live on."

Ibrahim, *full of curiosity, asked,* ***"So, if money isn't the goal, what should we aim for in life?"***

Great Grandpa smiled warmly. "Aim for a balanced life. Work hard, earn honestly, but never let money own you. Focus on building relationships, gaining knowledge, and helping others. True wealth is not in your bank account but in your heart. It's in the people who love you, the kindness you spread, and the peace you feel when you do the right thing. That, my dear children, is the real success in life."

The room fell silent for a moment as the children absorbed his words. Slowly, smiles spread across their faces. The world suddenly seemed a little clearer, a little less confusing. They had come seeking answers, and **Great Grandpa** had given them something far more valuable—a new way to look at life.

Maryam *nodded thoughtfully.* ***"So, money is important, but only as a means, not the purpose of life?"***

Great Grandpa nodded. *"Exactly! Let money serve you, not control you. Live simply, love deeply, and give generously. That is the true meaning of a peaceful and fulfilling life."*

The children exchanged glances, feeling wiser than before. Today's lesson was one they would carry in their hearts forever.

Yousuf: "Great Grandpa, ***in today's world, people believe that money equals happiness. But we see so many wealthy people who are still unhappy. Why is that?"***

Great Grandpa: "Ah, my dear **Yousuf,** money is a useful tool, but it was never meant to be the purpose of life. It can buy comfort, but not contentment. A full wallet doesn't guarantee a full heart."

Ibrahim: ***"But isn't financial stability important? How do we know how much is 'enough'?"***

Great Grandpa: "A wise man once said, 'Enough is when your needs are met, and your heart is at peace.' If you always want more, you will always feel poor. True wealth is the ability to sleep peacefully at night, knowing you owe nothing to anyone and have enough to sustain your life."

Maryam: ***"Many people borrow money and live beyond their means. Is debt dangerous, or is it sometimes necessary?"***

Great Grandpa: "Debt is like fire—it can be useful, but if not controlled, it will consume you. Borrow only what is needed, and always strive to live within your means."

Yousuf: ***"But some people become rich through dishonest means—cheating, corruption, or harming others. Is wealth meaningful if it comes at the cost of morals?"***

Great Grandpa: *"Wealth gained through dishonesty is like water held in your hands—it will slip away sooner or later. The real measure of a person's success is not how much money they have but how they earned it and how they use it."*

Ibrahim: ***"People today measure success by luxury—expensive cars, big houses, and designer clothes. Why has society become so obsessed with material things?"***

Great Grandpa: *"Because people confuse 'having more' with 'being more.' But tell me, does a golden cage make a bird free?"*

Maryam: *"**No, it only traps the bird in luxury.**"*

Great Grandpa: *"Exactly! The more we attach our happiness to possessions, the more we become prisoners of our desires."*

Yousuf: ***"Social media makes it even worse. Everyone feels pressured to show off. Does having more really bring satisfaction?"***

Great Grandpa: "Son, the heart is like a vessel—if you pour water into it endlessly, it will overflow, but it will never be full. The only way to fill the heart is with gratitude, not possessions."

Maryam: *"**How can we know when we've crossed the line from owning things for necessity to being trapped in materialism?**"*

Great Grandpa: "When what you own begins to own you. If your happiness depends on things, you are already trapped."

Ibrahim: ***"You lived in a simpler time than us. Were people happier back then?"***

Great Grandpa: "Happiness was not in the past, my dear—it is in simplicity. The less you complicate life, the more joy you will find."

Yousuf: ***"Great Grandpa, people today are more self-centered. Why is society becoming less caring?"***

Great Grandpa: "Because people have been taught that success means 'winning alone.' But real success is when you grow without pulling others down."

Maryam: ***"We see greed and selfishness even within families. How can we protect ourselves from becoming like that?"***

Great Grandpa: "Always remember: wealth disappears, beauty fades, but a good heart remains forever. Be the kind of person whose presence is a blessing to others, not a burden."

Ibrahim: ***"But in today's world, people say, 'If you are too kind, others will take advantage of you.' How do we balance kindness with self-protection?"***

Great Grandpa: "Kindness should have wisdom. Be generous, but don't let people use your goodness for their selfish gains. A wise heart knows when to give and when to say no."

Maryam: "You have always emphasized saving and avoiding extravagance. How can we develop the habit of financial discipline in an age of consumerism?"

Great-Grandpa:

Ah, **Maryam**, that's a very thoughtful question. Financial discipline is like planting a tree—you must nurture it patiently before you can enjoy its shade. In today's world, where advertisements tempt us at every turn, resisting unnecessary spending requires strong willpower and wisdom.

First, always differentiate between **needs and wants**. Needs are essentials—food, shelter, education—while wants are often just fleeting desires. If you master this distinction, half the battle is won.

Second, **follow a budget**. Even the wealthiest people set limits on their spending. Track your income and expenses, and always set aside a portion for savings before indulging in luxuries.

Third, **avoid debt traps**. Credit cards and easy loans may seem convenient, but they can silently enslave you. If you can't afford something today, ask yourself if it's worth sacrificing your financial peace in the future.

Fourth, **embrace simplicity**. A simple life brings more contentment than a lavish one. True happiness doesn't come from possessions but from meaningful relationships and inner peace.

Finally, **develop the habit of saving and investing wisely**. Set aside something regularly, even if it's a small amount. Over time, it will grow and become a safety net in times of need.

Remember, money is a tool—use it wisely, and it will serve you well. Let it control you, and you will always be chasing it.

Ibrahim: "Is it possible to live a good life without chasing a high-paying job or business? How do we define financial success without being obsessed with wealth?"

Great-Grandpa:
Ah, **Ibrahim**, that's a question filled with wisdom! Society often measures success by the size of one's paycheck or business empire, but true financial success is about stability, contentment, and a life free from constant worry.

A good life doesn't require chasing a high-paying job or a big business. It requires **financial wisdom, not just financial wealth**. Here's how:

1. **Live Within Your Means** – Wealth is not just about how much you earn, but how well you manage what you have. A person earning modestly but spending wisely will always be more secure

than someone earning millions but drowning in debt.

2. **Define Your Own Success** – True success is having enough to meet your needs, support your family, and live without financial stress. If you wake up with peace of mind, have food on your table, and sleep without worry, you are already richer than many.

3. **Focus on Purpose, Not Just Paychecks** – A high salary may not bring happiness if the job drains your soul. Choose work that gives you satisfaction, purpose, and balance. A teacher, a craftsman, or a farmer who loves his work and provides for his family is far more successful than a millionaire burdened by stress.

4. **Invest in Relationships, Not Just Wealth** – No amount of money can replace the warmth of family, the joy of friendship, or the peace of a content heart. True wealth is in strong relationships and good health.

5. **Seek Barakah, Not Just Numbers** – Money earned through honest, ethical means and spent wisely will always be more blessed than a fortune gained through greed. A small income with barakah (divine blessings) will stretch farther than a large income wasted on extravagance.

So, my dear **Ibrahim**, financial success is not about being the richest—it's about having **enough**, being **content**, and living **without fear of financial ruin**. Chase stability, not just wealth, and you will always live a good life.

Yousuf: *"We see billionaires who own everything but still feel empty inside. Why do people with less often seem happier than those with more?"*

Great Grandpa: Ah, Ibrahim, that is a profound observation. Many people believe that wealth brings happiness, but in reality, happiness and wealth are not always connected. True happiness comes from contentment, purpose, and inner peace, not from the number of possessions one owns.

Look at nature—does a bird own a mansion? Does it have a bank account? Yet, it sings every morning, free and full of joy. Now, look at billionaires who have everything money can buy but still feel restless, empty, and unsatisfied. Why?

1. The More You Have, the More You Worry – Wealth brings responsibilities, anxieties, and fears. Billionaires constantly think about protecting their wealth, growing their businesses, and staying ahead of competitors. In contrast, a person with just enough to live comfortably often sleeps peacefully.

2. Chasing the Unending Race – When people make wealth their goal, they never feel they have enough. They always want more—more money, more luxury, more power. But the problem is, desires have no limit. A man who drinks salty water to quench his thirst only becomes thirstier.

3. Loss of Simplicity and Gratitude – Those who less often appreciate small joys—a shared meal, a warm conversation, a peaceful evening with family. The wealthy, on the other hand, often lose touch with life's simple pleasures, constantly seeking bigger thrills that fail to satisfy them.

4. Relationships Over Riches – People with less often value their relationships more, while the ultra-rich sometimes lose true companionship. They suspect others of using them, struggle with trust, and may feel lonely despite being surrounded by people.

5. Barakah vs. Materialism – A small amount of wealth, earned honestly and spent wisely, brings peace and fulfillment. But an abundance of wealth without gratitude or purpose becomes a burden. That's why a farmer who works in his field with a grateful

heart might be far happier than a millionaire trapped in board meetings and endless stress.

So, **Ibrahim**, wealth itself is not the enemy, but obsession with wealth is. True happiness comes from contentment, gratitude, faith, and strong relationships—not from riches alone. A heart at peace is richer than a vault full of gold.

A Message for the Next Generation

Maryam: *"Great Grandpa, you have seen different generations and lived through changing times. What is the secret to living a simple, worry-free, and peaceful life?"*

Great Grandpa: Ah, my dear **Maryam**, that is a question filled with wisdom—one that takes a lifetime to truly understand. The key to a simple, worry-free, and peaceful life lies in contentment, gratitude, and balance. These are not just words but a way of living.

To embrace this life fully, keep these guiding principles close to your heart:

1. Live within your means – Never chase after what you cannot afford or what is beyond your needs. Simplicity brings peace.
2. Be grateful – Appreciate what you have rather than lament what you don't. A heart filled with gratitude has no room for worries.
3. Keep faith and trust in the Almighty – Accept that not everything is in our control. Do your best, and leave the rest to Him.
4. Stay away from unnecessary conflicts – Avoid arguments, especially those that serve no purpose but to hurt others or your own peace of mind.
5. Take care of your health – A simple lifestyle with good food, fresh air, and some physical activity keeps the body and mind at ease.
6. Maintain strong family bonds – Love, respect, and spend time with your family. The warmth of relationships is the greatest wealth.
7. Let go of the past – Worries often come from regrets. Learn from the past, but don't carry its burdens.

8. Be kind and help others – A helping hand brings inner peace like nothing else.

A simple life is not about having less, my dear—it's about needing less and appreciating more.

Yousuf: ***"Is it possible to be financially stable without being consumed by greed? How do we find the balance between earning for our needs and avoiding the constant race for more?"***

Great Grandpa: Ah, **Yousuf,** financial stability and greed are two different things. It is absolutely possible to be financially stable without being consumed by greed—if you understand the difference between needs and wants. To navigate this wisely, consider these guiding principles:

1. Earn with honesty – Wealth earned ethically brings true peace. If money comes through deception or greed, it becomes a burden.
2. Live with moderation – Don't spend beyond your means, and don't hoard unnecessarily. Earn what is enough for a comfortable life, not to show off.
3. Save wisely, but don't be miserly – A portion of your earnings should be saved for the future, but also spent on the present with gratitude.
4. Give charity (Zakat, Sadaqah) – The more you help others, the more blessings come into your own life. Wealth is a test; use it wisely.
5. Don't chase wealth at the cost of family, health, or faith – True stability is not just financial but also emotional and spiritual.

The balance lies in earning enough to live comfortably while understanding that excess wealth does not bring true happiness—contentment does.

Ibrahim: ***"What daily habits can help us live a life of peace and contentment in this fast-moving, stressful world?"***

Great Grandpa: My dear **Ibrahim**, peace and contentment in today's fast-moving world come from discipline and simplicity in daily habits. Here are a few things that help:

1. Start the day with prayer and gratitude – It sets the right mindset for the day.
2. Have a simple and healthy routine – Eat well, get enough sleep, and engage in some physical activity.
3. Limit unnecessary distractions – Too much social media, news, or negative influences bring stress.
4. Spend quality time with family – A peaceful heart comes from strong relationships, not from busy schedules.
5. Do one good deed every day – Even a small act of kindness brings inner joy.
6. Stay away from unnecessary worries – Focus on what you can control, and leave the rest to the Almighty.
7. End the day with reflection – Ask yourself, "Did I live today in a way that brings peace to my heart?" If yes, sleep with contentment.

The key is not letting the world's speed dictate your peace—slow down, breathe, and live purposefully.

Maryam: *"If we don't find happiness in money, fame, or possessions, then where does real happiness come from?"*

Great Grandpa: Ah, my dear **Maryam**, as I have often told you, real happiness is not found in money, fame, or possessions—these are fleeting illusions. The more you chase them, the more they slip away, leaving you wanting even more. True happiness is not something you acquire; it is something you cultivate from within. It blossoms in:

1. Gratitude – Appreciating what you already have instead of focusing on what you lack.
2. Strong relationships – The love of family, the company of true friends, and the joy of giving to others bring lasting happiness.

3. Faith and trust in the Almighty – When you believe that everything happens for a reason, your heart remains at peace.
4. Purpose and contentment – Doing meaningful work, helping others, and being satisfied with what you have.

Remember, happiness is not in having more, but in needing less and appreciating more.

Yousuf: *"You always tell us that inner peace is more important than material success. But how do we achieve that peace when the world around us is full of stress and competition?"*

Great Grandpa: Ah, **Yousuf,** you are right—the world is full of stress and competition. But peace is not something that the world gives you; it is something you create within yourself. Here's how to achieve inner peace:

1. Detach from unnecessary worries – Don't let the fear of the future or regrets of the past steal your present peace.
2. Live with purpose, not comparison – Focus on your own journey, not what others are doing. Compete with yourself, not the world.
3. Keep your heart pure – Avoid grudges, envy, and hatred. Forgiveness brings peace, while negativity brings stress.
4. Simplify your life – The less you complicate things, the more peace you will find. Live simply, think positively.
5. Trust the Almighty's plan – Do your best, then leave the rest to Him. Peace comes when you surrender unnecessary control.

Inner peace is a choice, my dear—it is not about changing the world, but about changing how you react to it.

Ibrahim: *"If you could give us one golden rule to follow for a life filled with peace, meaning, and contentment, what would it be?"*

Great Grandpa: Ah, my dear **Ibrahim**, if I could give you just one golden rule for a life of peace, meaning, and contentment, it would be this:

👉 "Live in the present, with gratitude and trust in the Almighty."

- The past is gone—learn from it, but don't carry its burden.
- The future is unknown—prepare for it, but don't fear it.
- The present moment is all you truly have—make it beautiful by being grateful, kind, and content.

A peaceful life is not about having no problems, my dear—it's about having the right mindset to handle them with patience and faith.

More Personal Reflections

Great-Grandchildren: ***Great-Grandpa, we hope you don't mind, but our next questions are quite personal. Would you be okay if we ask them?***
Great-Grandpa: Haha! My dear ones, at my age, there's nothing to hide. Go ahead—ask whatever is in your heart. I promise to answer with honesty and a smile!

Maryam: ***Great-Grandpa, you've shared so much wisdom with us. But tell me, how do you feel when you look back at your life?***

Great-Grandpa: Ah, my dear, life feels like a river—constantly flowing, never stopping. When I look back, I see moments of joy, struggles, achievements, and regrets. But most of all, I feel grateful. Grateful for the love I received, the lessons I learned, and the legacy I hope to leave behind.

Maryam: ***Do you think life was better in your time or now?***

Great-Grandpa: Every era has its blessings and challenges. In my time, life was simpler—people valued relationships more, families were close, and respect for elders was strong. But today, life is faster, technology connects us in ways we never imagined, and knowledge is at our fingertips. Yet, despite all the advancements, I sometimes feel people are lonelier than before. Balance is the key, my dear.

Maryam: ***If you could change one thing about your past, what would it be?***

Great-Grandpa: Perhaps, I would have spent even more time with my loved ones. In youth, we chase careers and ambitions, thinking we have plenty of time. But as years pass, we realize that time with family is the most precious gift.

Cultural and Religious Perspectives

Ibrahim: Great-Grandpa, ***you have lived in different cultures and seen different traditions. How do culture and religion shape a person's life?***

Great-Grandpa: My dear, culture is like the clothes we wear, and religion is the light that guides our path. Both shape our identity, values, and way of thinking. Living in different cultures has taught me that, despite our differences, all humans seek love, peace, and a meaningful life.

Ibrahim: ***But why do people sometimes fight over religion and culture?***

Great-Grandpa: Because they forget the essence of both. Religion teaches us kindness, patience, and justice, but people often misuse it for personal gain. Culture should bring people together, not divide them. The best way is to learn from every culture while staying true to one's values.

Ibrahim: ***What is the most valuable lesson religion has taught you?***

Great-Grandpa: That everything in life—wealth, health, even time—is temporary. We are travelers in this world, and our true success lies in how we treat others, help the less fortunate, and remain grateful to our Creator.

A Nice Closing Chapter: The Final Conversation

Yousuf: ***Great-Grandpa, if you could leave me with just one piece of advice for life, what would it be?***

Great-Grandpa: My dear, remember this—live a life of purpose. Don't just exist; make a difference. Be kind, seek knowledge, help others, and always stay connected to your roots.

Yousuf: ***Will I always have your wisdom to guide me?***

Great-Grandpa: My wisdom will live in you, in these conversations, and in the values I have passed on. And when you grow old, share these lessons with your grandchildren. This is how wisdom travels through time.

Yousuf: ***That means our conversations will never truly end, right?***

Great-Grandpa: Yes, my dear. As long as you remember them, they will live on forever.

All three together: ***"Great Grandpa, if today were the last day you could give us advice, what is the most important thing you want us to remember?"***

Great Grandpa (smiling):
"My dear **children**, life is a fleeting journey. Love deeply, give generously, live simply, and trust that true success is not measured by what you have, but by the hearts you touch."

The conversation had been long and deeply meaningful for the **great-grandchildren**. It was a discussion that left everyone reflecting on life, yet paradoxically, it revolved around the very essence of keeping stress away. Their young minds were brimming with thoughts, ideas, and the invaluable wisdom of their **Great-Grandpa**, who had guided them on how to live a fulfilling present and a hopeful future. But now, the sun had already begun its descent, and the **great-grandfather** looked visibly exhausted. As was his tradition, he gently announced that today's conversation was adjourned and that they would gather again the following weekend.

The **great-grandchildren**, however, had a secret plan—a grand, heartfelt celebration for their beloved **Great-Grandpa**'s 100th birthday, just hours away. The milestone moment would arrive the next morning—Sunday—a day destined to be filled with love, laughter, and a surprise that would leave their Great-Grandpa speechless.

As soon as their cozy evening conversation ended, they exchanged knowing glances and dashed upstairs, their little hearts pounding with excitement. Whispering and giggling, they meticulously crafted every detail of the surprise. Their eyes sparkled with mischief as they urged their parents to make a last-minute dash to Costco—there was no celebration without a grand, colorful cake! And for their cherished **Great-Grandpa**, they had chosen the perfect gifts—an elegant long coat and a warm, furry hat, a symbol of their love and gratitude for the man who had given them a lifetime of wisdom and stories.

The night stretched on, but sleep was the last thing on their minds. Tiny hands worked tirelessly—cutting, gluing, hanging decorations, wrapping gifts with clumsy yet loving care, and rehearsing songs that would bring happy tears to their **Great-Grandpa**'s eyes. Excitement buzzed in the air like a secret melody only they could hear.

Yet, amidst all the flurry of preparations, their **Great-Grandpa** remained blissfully unaware. He sat in his favorite chair, lost in thought, gazing at the clock ticking away the last few hours of his 99th year. He had, in fact, forgotten that he was about to cross a once-in-a-lifetime threshold—a century of life, love, and memories.

Little did he know, tomorrow would bring a moment he would never forget—one filled with laughter, happy tears, and the warmth of a family's love wrapped around him like a precious gift.

Session Ten

Great Grandpa's Journey Through Time—A Tale of Imagination and Reality

"From Past to Future"

"Countdown to 100! Celebrating a Century of Love, Laughter, and Great Grandpa's Incredible Life!"

As usual, **Great-Grandpa** woke up early the next morning, but something was different. A strange weakness had settled over him. He felt unusually lethargic, his body heavy with exhaustion. Even after performing his morning prayers, he lacked the energy to take his daily morning walk. The crisp morning air, his usual attire, and his walking stick—all remained untouched. Instead, he settled into his favorite armchair in the family room, staring at nothing, his thoughts wandering. Eventually, he mustered the will to make himself a cup of black coffee. He carefully carried his steaming mug back to his chair, but even as he sipped, the familiar bitterness failed to awaken his senses.

Just then, something unexpected happened. **Lucy**, the little family pet, appeared before him at an unusual hour, escaping the watchful eyes of **Maryam, Ibrahim, and Yousuf**. **Great-Grandpa** looked at her, surprised. He lifted her onto his lap and gently stroked her fur. **Lucy** nestled in his arms as if sensing something was amiss. He took another sip of coffee, lost in thought, while the house upstairs buzzed with secret excitement.

Happy 100th Birthday to Great Grandpa:

Time passed swiftly. Finally, the moment arrived. A whisper grew into a loud, joyful chorus: **"Happy Birthday, Great-Grandpa**!" The children descended the stairs in a lively dance, carrying balloons, streamers, and their carefully wrapped gifts. The grand drawing room was beautifully decorated; a single-seated sofa was adorned especially for the guest of honor. Everything was set for the celebration, but amidst the flurry of excitement, one small detail went unnoticed—**Lucy** was missing.

Maryam rushed upstairs to find her, but **Lucy** was nowhere to be seen. Meanwhile, **Yousuf** and **Ibrahim** silently made their way to the family room, expecting to greet their **Great-Grandpa** with hugs and cheers. With wide smiles, they called out, “Good morning, **Great-Grandpa**! **Happy Birthday**, our darling **Great-Grandpa**!” But there was no response. They giggled, thinking he was playing a trick on them. However, as they approached, their laughter froze. The coffee cup lay on the floor, its contents spilled across the rug. **Great-Grandpa** sat still, his face peaceful yet unresponsive. **Lucy** remained curled in his lap, as if guarding a sacred moment.

"The Day Everything Stopped: Great Grandpa’s Cardiac Arrest and the Shocking Moment His Great-Grandchildren Will Never Forget"

A chilling realization settled over them like a heavy fog. Their hands trembled as they reached out, shaking him, calling his name—again and again—desperation rising with each unanswered plea. Tears blurred their vision, their cries slicing through the silence of the house, raw and frantic.

Footsteps thundered down the hallway. Their parents burst in, eyes wide with fear, and within moments, a phone was in hand—911 dialed with shaky fingers. Sirens pierced the night air, growing louder, faster, until red and blue lights painted the walls in a frantic dance.

Paramedics stormed in, their movements swift, precise—urgency crackling in the air. **Cardiac arrest.** The words struck like a hammer. The children stood frozen, clutching each other, their tiny hands clasped in silent, desperate prayer as the battle for life unfolded before them.

CPR. Chest compressions. Nothing. A stretcher. A blur of movement. And then, in the ambulance, the final gamble—the defibrillator. A shock. Then another. A desperate attempt to reignite the spark that was slipping, fading, drifting beyond reach.

And then—a miracle.

The ambulance sped through the morning, sirens wailing, as if urging time itself to move faster. Inside, paramedics worked with unwavering focus, their hands steady, their voices firm. In the car trailing behind, the children sat in breathless silence, their wide eyes fixed on the flashing lights ahead. Their parents gripped the wheel tightly, whispering silent prayers with every passing second.

At the hospital, **Great-Grandpa** was rushed into the ICU, swallowed by a flurry of doctors and nurses. Machines beeped, monitors flickered, and for a moment, everything hung in unbearable suspense.

Then—a sharp intake of breath.

His frail chest rose, a flicker of life returning. His pulse, though weak, persisted. The doctors didn't pause, fighting to stabilize him, administering medications, and monitoring every sign of recovery. And then, ever so slightly, his eyelids fluttered open. His parched lips parted, and in a whisper, like a ghost of his former strength, he called out, **"Maryam... Ibrahim... Yousuf..."**

But the children weren't there to hear him. They stood outside the emergency ward, their small hands clasped together, their hearts pounding against their ribs. Every passing second felt like an eternity.

Then, the doors swung open. A kind-faced nurse stepped out, her voice soft yet steady. She knelt to their level, placing a gentle hand on **Maryam's** shoulder.

"Your **Great-Grandpa** is okay now. He just needs to rest. Keep praying for his strength."

Relief crashed over them like a tidal wave. **Maryam** choked back a sob. **Ibrahim** exhaled shakily. **Yousuf** pressed his palms together, whispering a silent prayer.

Great-Grandpa had come back to them. Now, all they could do was hope. And wait

With tears of relief, the children embraced the nurse, pleading to see him. "Not yet," she said, stroking their hair. "Give him time to recover."

That morning, the children returned home in a daze. The house, which had been alive with plans of joy, now felt hollow. They refused Lunch and dinner. Sleep eluded them. Even **Lucy**, who usually curled up contentedly, lay restless, her eyes brimming with silent sorrow. The night stretched on, filled with whispered prayers and quiet tears.

Morning came, heavy with anticipation. As soon as they arrived at the hospital, they were greeted with hopeful news—**Great-Grandpa** was stable. The duty nurse secured permission for them to visit, but only for five minutes. Shoes removed, hearts pounding, they stepped into the ICU.

The sight of him brought an overwhelming wave of emotions. **Great-Grandpa**, now awake, stretched out his arms, welcoming them into a warm embrace. They ran to him, sobbing into his chest, feeling the steady beat of his heart—a rhythm they had feared was lost forever.

But fate had one final twist.

As they clung to him, **Great-Grandpa** suddenly slumped back onto the bed. His arms, once wrapped around them with love, loosened their grip. **Maryam** was the first to notice. "**Great-Grandpa**?" she whispered, shaking him gently. No response.

Panic erupted. Doctors and nurses rushed in, ushering the children out. The machines beeped frantically. The doctors fought hard, trying every possible measure to bring him back. Minutes turned into an hour. But then—a final silence.

Great-Grandpa ***was gone. He left without a goodbye — just love behind. He had taken his final journey.***

Peacefully, in the embrace of his beloved **great-grandchildren**, he had taken his final journey—to a realm beyond pain, beyond time. The hospital walls bore witness to the cries of his grieving family. The celebration they had so carefully planned had transformed into the deepest sorrow of their lives.

This is the undeniable law of nature—every soul is destined to return to its Creator at a time and place known only to Him, written in secrecy beyond human understanding.

His body, still warm, still gentle, was placed in their care. Those same hands, once strong enough to lift them high into the air, yet soft enough to wipe away their tears, now lay motionless. Hands that had guided them, blessed them, and held them through every joy and sorrow. Now, they rested in eternal stillness.

With heavy hearts and trembling steps, they accompanied him on his final journey. Dar-Us-Salaam Cemetery in San Jose, California, became his resting place, a sanctuary where the love of those he had touched gathered one last time. Prayers whispered through the air, mixing with quiet sobs, as he was laid to rest beneath the endless sky.

And so, the conversations between **Great-Grandpa** and his **great-grandchildren** came to an end. A silence followed—one so deep, so vast, that it left a void no words could ever fill. Yet, his presence remained, woven into their memories, etched into their hearts. His laughter, his wisdom, his unwavering love—these would never fade. They would live on, shaping their lives, guiding their steps, whispering to them in moments of doubt.

Though he had completed a century, the grand celebration they had envisioned never came to life. No candles flickered, no cake was sliced, no cheers of joy filled the air. Instead, the day unfolded as a solemn yet powerful tribute—one that needed no festivity to mark its significance. It became a quiet reflection of a life richly lived, a love profoundly shared, and a bond so deep that even death could not sever it.

But one question still lingered, hanging in the air like an unfinished melody.

"Great-Grandpa, ***if today were the last day you could give us advice, what is the most important thing you want us to remember?"***

At the time, they had asked it playfully, never imagining it would be his final lesson to them. But now, as they stood outside the ICU, hearts pounding, eyes swollen from tears, his answer carried a weight they never could have foreseen.

His last words—spoken with warmth, with wisdom, with a love that had stretched across generations—returned to them, wrapping around their souls like a final embrace.

"**My dear children, life is a fleeting journey. Love deeply, give generously, live simply, and trust that true success is not measured by what you have, but by the hearts you touch."**

It was as if he had known. As if, in that moment, he had been preparing them for what was to come.

Maryam pressed her fists against her chest, fighting the sob that threatened to escape. **Ibrahim** swallowed hard, his breath hitching as the words replayed in his mind. **Yousuf**, the youngest, wiped his tear-streaked face, whispering the advice over and over, afraid to let even a single syllable slip away.

The weight of his wisdom was now theirs to carry. His legacy was no longer just in the stories he had told but in the love he had left behind.

And as they stood there, beneath the vast sky that now cradled his soul, they held onto his final gift, vowing never to forget.

A deep, unbridgeable void now lingers between the **great-grandchildren** and their beloved **great-grandfather**—a space that time itself may never mend. The echoes of his absence haunt their young hearts, etching an irreplaceable emptiness into their souls. The most painful truth is that they never got to hear his final words, his last wishes—words that would have been his farewell, his blessing, his love wrapped in parting whispers. Before they could hold his hand one last time, he had already embarked on a journey from which no traveler returns. And just like that, the beautiful chapter of togetherness between a **great-grandfather** and his **great-grandchildren** came to its inevitable, heartbreaking end.

Last Session

"A Heartfelt Reunion After 30 Years: Navigating the Shadows of Time to Embrace the Light of Togetherness"

Great Grandpa's Absence Leaves a Deep Void in His Great-Grandchildren's Hearts

Laid to Rest with Love at Dar-Us-Salaam Cemetery, San Jose, California

Time flowed like a river, carrying with it the days, months, and years. Three decades passed in the blink of an eye, and the children who once played in the warmth of their **great-grandfathe**r's embrace had now grown into remarkable individuals. Life had taken them on different paths, yet fate orchestrated a heartfelt reunion at Monte Lindo Court, San Jose, California. They had now established their own families, stepping into the very roles their elders once held.

The house, once a radiant sanctuary of love and laughter, now stood cloaked in an aching silence, its very soul longing for the warmth and joy of days gone by. The once-vibrant walls, rich with stories and colors that welcomed every heart, had faded into somber, lifeless shades as if time itself had swept away their brilliance. The long, flowing curtains that once danced in playful harmony with the wind, echoing the giggles of **great-grandchildren**, now hung still and weary, stripped of their charm, missing the tiny hands that once tugged at them with innocent delight.

Every piece of furniture bore the weight of loneliness—its hues dulled, its polished surfaces now veiled beneath a layer of neglect. The beloved armchair of **Great-Grandpa**, once a throne of wisdom and warmth, sat there in sorrow, its faded, pale-yellow fabric seeming to whisper in quiet desperation, searching for the one who had spent countless hours nestled in its embrace. Even the grand chandelier, once the crowning jewel of the home, had dimmed, Its diamond glow faded to a soft, sorrowful flicker, as if mourning the absence of the man whose laughter had once echoed through the halls like a cherished melody, now lost to time.

And then there was Lucy—the little kitten whose soft "Mao Mao" had once been a symphony of love in the house. But now, her sweet echoes had vanished, just like her tiny paws that once scampered through the rooms. She, too, had left this world after **Great-Grandpa's** passing, as if her heart could not bear the emptiness he left behind. The home, now shrouded in an unspeakable stillness, grieved not just the loss of its guardian but also the absence of all that made it truly alive.

A strange emptiness loomed in the air, as though the house itself was mourning the void left behind. The peaceful atmosphere it once radiated now felt incomplete—stripped of the energy of children running, playing, and filling every corner with their boundless joy. Outside, the front garden, which once bloomed in a riot of colors, now stood in a state of dull desolation. The roses, once blushing with life, had lost their vibrance, their petals whispering tales of an era gone by. In the backyard, the fruit trees—Persimmon, Apple, Pear, Peach, Pomegranate, and Lemon—once lush and full of life, now stood weary, their charm diminished, their greenery retreating as if in silent grief.

The deafening silence inside and outside the house was a haunting reminder of the legacy of familyhood that once flourished within these walls. The parents of the **great-grandchildren** had aged, their faces now bearing the lines of time, their eyes reflecting the longing for voices that once filled the air. The echoes of laughter, the playful mischief, the warmth of togetherness—all had become distant memories, leaving the house a mere shadow of its former self.

Time had weaved its inevitable truth into every brick, every creaking floorboard, every faded hue of the home. The once-vivid beauty of this place had become a relic of the past—a silent storyteller of history, whispering the bittersweet truth of life. Everything, no matter how radiant, must eventually succumb to the music of decay and death. It is the unspoken decree of the Creator—a profound reminder that all things, no matter how cherished, must face their final dusk before surrendering to the eternal passage of time.

Dr. **Maryam**, the little girl who once sat on her **great-grandfather'**s lap listening to his stories, had blossomed into a distinguished oncologist. She earned her MBBS and completed her Master's in Oncology from Ludwig Maximilian University of Munich, Germany followed by a Ph.D. from the same institution. Today, she stands as one of the finest oncologists in Munich, a visiting consultant at MD Anderson Cancer Center in Houston, and a pioneer in epidemiological research. With her husband, also a doctor in the same discipline, she built a life in Munich, raising a beautiful daughter and a bright young son. Despite the miles that separated them, she never failed to visit San Jose once a year to see her aging parents, cherishing the warmth of home.

Ibrahim, once a curious little boy who built toy rockets in his backyard, had turned his childhood fascination into a lifelong mission. He graduated with a Bachelor of Science in Aerospace Engineering from MIT, Cambridge, Massachusetts, USA followed by a Master's from the same prestigious institution. Now, his research at CALTECH (California Institute of Technology) Fuels his ultimate dream—to contribute to NASA's Mars Exploration Program in Houston, Texas. His wife, a brilliant scientist working with SpaceX on Elon Musk's Mars mission, shared his vision of establishing a human colony on the Red Planet. Together, they were raising two young boys, instilling in them the same passion for the cosmos that once filled **Ibrahim**'s own heart. They are driven by a bold ambition—to be part of a historic manned mission to Mars, venturing into the unknown and shaping the future of space exploration.

Yousuf, the youngest of the three, evolved from a curious child into a visionary technological pioneer. Armed with a Bachelor's and Master's in Computer Science from MIT, Cambridge, Massachusetts, USA, he pushed the boundaries of Machine Learning research at Harvard's Graduate School. Together with his equally brilliant wife, he explored the limitless possibilities of artificial intelligence while nurturing their bright young daughter, who shared his insatiable hunger for knowledge.

With a PhD in Machine Learning, **Yousuf** set his sights on a mission far beyond personal success: revolutionizing global governance. He envisioned a world where AI-driven robotics could oversee and guide the parliaments of great nations, eliminating bias, corruption, and inefficiency. His ultimate goal was nothing short of historic: to create a future where reason triumphed over greed, conflicts became relics of the past, and Earth thrived in an era of lasting peace.

Their parents, now retired, found solace in social welfare activities, spending their golden years giving back to the community. Yet, their greatest joy lay in the rare moments they could visit their children, sharing stories with their grandchildren—just as their grandfather had once done.

Despite their success, the three siblings never forgot the man who had shaped their dreams—their beloved **Great-Grandpa**. Though he was no longer in this world, his wisdom, love, and unwavering faith lived on in their hearts. They firmly believed that his soul rested in Barzakh (a place where souls wait until the day of Judgment), finding peace in the achievements of his **great-grandchildren**.

As time moved forward, one milestone brought them together again—the 130th birth anniversary of their **Great-Grandpa**. This was not merely a celebration, but a solemn pilgrimage to honor his memory. With heavy hearts, they gathered at Dar-Us-Salaam Cemetery in San Jose on a crisp autumn morning. The golden leaves whispered in the gentle breeze, mirroring the unspoken sorrow in their hearts. Each carried a bouquet of fresh roses, their eyes brimming with unshed tears, lips trembling with silent prayers.

For the first time, **Great-Grandpa** was not there to greet them with his twinkling eyes and warm chuckles. There was no steaming cup of coffee in his hands, no soothing voice weaving old tales into the morning air. The house felt different—quieter, heavier—his absence lingering like an unspoken whisper in every corner, like a melody suddenly missing its most cherished note.

But though his body now rested beneath the earth, wrapped in eternal peace, his soul had merely transitioned to another realm—the unseen world of ***Barzakh***. A realm shrouded in mystery, where souls linger between the known and the unknown, waiting for the dawn of the Day of Judgment.

In Islamic belief, ***Barzakh*** is not merely a resting place but a passage—an enigmatic bridge between life and the eternal, where the constraints of time dissolve, and the illusions of the mortal world fade. It is a dimension beyond human perception, untouched by the living, where no traveler has ever returned to reveal its secrets. Is it a sanctuary of serenity and divine mercy, or a domain of reflection and reckoning? The answer remains locked in silence, known only to those who have crossed its threshold.

Yet, even in this unseen world, love knows no bounds. Perhaps, in the stillness of *Barzakh*, his soul smiled—a quiet, knowing smile—watching over them with boundless pride and affection, whispering unseen blessings upon those he left behind.

A profound silence blanketed the cemetery, broken only by the whispering wind rustling through the trees—as if nature itself mourned his passing. The weight of the moment hung heavy in the air, a silent reminder of the journey every soul must one day embark upon. His **great-great-grandchildren**, too young to grasp the gravity of death, clung to their parents' hands. Their innocent eyes, filled with wonder rather than sorrow, followed the dry leaves as they danced with the wind, longing to chase them, unaware of the solemnity surrounding them.

Great Grandchildren *knelt beside the grave, their voices trembling as they whispered heartfelt prayers, seeking Allah's (God,s) boundless mercy upon their beloved* **Great-Grandpa**. *They prayed for his soul's journey through Barzakh—the mysterious realm where all must pass but none have ever returned to tell its truths. Is it a realm of peace, bathed in* *divine light, or a space where souls long and reflect on their earthly deeds? No one knows. No voice has ever echoed back from that world, no eyes have seen and returned to describe its depths. It remains the greatest enigma of existence—the veil between this life and the eternal one beyond.*

And yet, in their hearts, they clung to faith. They believed, as he had, that beyond this silence, beyond this resting place, lay a reunion with divine mercy—a journey leading to *Jannah (Heaven)*, where souls would find eternal peace. The setting sun cast golden hues over his resting place, as if whispering a silent promise: though his body now lay beneath the earth, his soul had merely crossed into the unseen. One day, they too would follow—not into darkness, but into the light of eternity, where love never fades and where, at last, all hearts would be whole again.

As the sun began its descent, casting golden hues upon the sky, the family stood together, gazing at the grave one last time. With heavy hearts and tear-filled eyes, they waved—Not in farewell, but in an eternal promise.

A promise to keep his legacy alive. A promise to carry forward his teachings. A promise to reunite with him once again—on a day only Allah (God) knows.

And so, they turned away, walking into the horizon, leaving behind a piece of their hearts but carrying with them the lessons and love of a great man who would forever live in their souls.

And so, the cherished sessions of ***Conversations with My Great-Grandchildren*** draw to a poignant close—leaving behind a treasure trove of laughter, wisdom, and love. The once vibrant exchanges, brimming with curiosity and wonder, gradually give way to silence, a silence heavy with the unspoken ache of parting. The warmth of shared stories still lingers in the air, yet a quiet sorrow settles in as if even time itself grieves the end of this beautiful chapter. But though the voices may fade, the memories remain—etched not only in their hearts but in the very fabric of their souls, destined to be carried forward, whispered from one generation to the next.

As I reach the final words of this book, I can almost feel the silent reflection of those who have journeyed through its pages. To you, **the reader**, who has embraced the wisdom of **Great Grandpa**, laughed at his wit, and pondered the brilliance of his **great-grandchildren**'s questions—this moment must feel like partying with an old friend.

The wise storyteller, whose voice once filled these pages with warmth and insight, may no longer be here, but his wisdom lingers, woven into every lesson, every story, and every heartfelt conversation. His **great-grandchildren**, with their sharp minds and boundless curiosity, breathed life into these discussions, turning simple questions into profound revelations, leaving behind wisdom not just for themselves, but for all who listen.

And now, as the echoes of their conversations fade into memory, I know that some of you may feel a quiet sorrow—the kind that comes when something beautiful reaches its end. But perhaps, this is not an end at all. For as long as these stories are read, as long as their lessons touch hearts, **Great Grandpa's** voice will never truly fade.

May his wisdom live on in you, **the reader**—in your thoughts, in your questions, and in the way you embrace the wonder of life.

A Writer's Journey: Behind the Making of This Book

Is it fiction... or a fragment of truth wrapped in love? Only your heart can decide.

Every book begins somewhere. Some are born in crowded cafés, others in the quiet corners of writing desks. But this book—***Conversations with My Great Grandchildren: Fiction or Fact?***—was not born in a place. It was born in moments. In laughter-filled mornings and wonder-filled evenings. In bedtime questions that refused simple answers. In the twinkling eyes of three little souls—**Mariyam**, **Ibrahim**, and **Yousuf**—whose innocence gently shattered my adult world, only to rebuild it with their pure, unfiltered curiosity.

This is not just a book. This is my legacy, inked with love, stitched with emotion, and sealed with the silent prayers of an aging heart.

The idea didn't appear like a flash of lightning. It bloomed slowly—like a flower that takes its time to face the sun. Night after night, sitting with my grandchildren, I found myself marveling at their questions. Simple? Yes. But beneath their simplicity lay depth. "Why do people die?" "Where do dreams go?" "Why do some people hurt others?" Questions that made me pause... smile... cry. Questions that made me human again.

In those sacred exchanges, I found the spark to write—not just answers, but a mirror to our shared curiosity. Not lectures, but heartfelt conversations. A child's curiosity is pure; I wanted to preserve that purity in these pages.

For decades, I was a mechanical engineer—a man of turbines, tools, and timelines. Writing was never on my blueprint. But retirement gave me something rare: stillness. And in that stillness, memories rose like forgotten stars. Words came, slowly at first, like hesitant footsteps... until they began to run.

And yet, it wasn't easy. Doubts whispered in the dark: *Who will read the musings of an old man?* But then I reminded myself—this book is not for the masses. It is for *them*. For my great-grandchildren. For every child who still asks why. For every grandparent who still listens. For you—dear reader—who still believes in the power of heartfelt stories.

The beauty of this book lies in its form. It is not a lecture; it's a legacy. It is not a sermon; it's a soul's song. The stories unfold through dialogue—sometimes playful, sometimes profound—between a **great-grandfather** and his inquisitive companions. We speak of love and loss, science and soul, faith and fear, health and dreams, war and peace, life and beyond.

Some stories are based in reality. Others take wings and fly into fiction. But all of them are wrapped in emotion, truth, and longing. They carry the weight of lived experience and the lightness of childhood dreams.

Writing this was a journey through time. I revisited my own childhood, walked through the alleys of memory, and marveled at how the world has changed. Yet the heart—ah, the heart remains the same. We all seek the same things: love, understanding, and stories that make us feel *we belong*.

And then… there were the chapters that shattered me.

When writing the passages about today's world—wars, injustice, destruction, the cruelty of leaders—I had to stop. My hands trembled. My eyes flooded. There were times I couldn't bear to continue. I had to leave my desk, retreat to the washroom, and sob silently. Those tears weren't just mine. They belonged to every child born into a world where peace is no longer promised.

But the hardest parts… they nearly broke me.

Writing the scene of the **great-grandfather's** heart attack—his collapse, his final farewell—was like living my own goodbye. I imagined the children's cries, their innocence colliding with irreversible loss, their trembling hands holding on to hope in a sterile hospital room. I wept every time I edited those lines. Not once, not twice—but at least twenty times. Each revision was a wound reopened. Each tear was real.

And then came the most soul-stirring passage—the one that quietly broke me.

The **great-grandchildren**, now standing at the summit of their careers, returned to visit the final resting place of their **Great Grandpa**—three decades after his passing. What began as a tribute became a storm of emotions I never saw coming.

They stood in silence by the grave, matured by time but still carrying the echoes of childhood wonder. Their heads bowed in prayer, their eyes moist with unspoken love, their hearts heavy with memories of stories once told under starlit skies. It was not just a visit—it was a reunion of souls across time.

Their whispered words, their trembling hands gently placing flowers on the tombstone, and the ache in their voices as they remembered the man who once filled their lives with tales, laughter, and dreams... it pierced through me in a way I cannot fully explain.

Even now, as I write this, that ache lingers in my chest. The gravity of that scene—the raw tenderness of it—took me ten long days to write, revise, and revisit. Each sentence pulled me deeper into emotion. Controlling my tears as I described it was perhaps the hardest part of the entire book.

This is not just a book, dear reader. It is my heart laid bare. It is a collection of memories, dreams, fears, and faith—woven into fiction, rooted in truth.

Now that it is in your hands, I feel a quiet peace. Perhaps it will bring a smile to your lips. Perhaps it will stir something within you. Perhaps it will start a conversation between you and someone you love.

And if it does, then my journey was worth it.

With gratitude,
M.N. Ashraf
Grandpa (as ***Great-Grandfather), Storyteller, Dreamer***

A Note to My Precious Great-Grandchildren Maryam, Ibrahim, and Yousuf

My dearest little stars,

As I close this book, I open my heart to you.

This is more than just a collection of stories. It is a quiet place where our laughter echoes, our questions live on, and our imaginations still run wild together. Every word is a thread in the fabric of memories we've shared, stitched with love, wonder, and a few giggles too.

Someday, when I may no longer be sitting beside you — to answer your curious questions, to play your favorite games, or to tell you stories at bedtime — may these pages remind you of how deeply you were loved.

And when you flip through them again, may you hear your **great-grandfather's** voice, gently whispering from the corners of time, guiding you with love, mischief, and a sparkle in the eye.

Never stop asking.
Never stop dreaming.
And above all, never stop being kind.

With all my love,
Your **Great Grandpa**

The Last Page, But Not the End

Every story worth telling eventually finds its final page—but the impact of its words, if true and heartfelt, can last a lifetime. This book was never just about a **great-grandfather** or his bright, curious **great-grandchildren**. It was about *us all*—the generations that seek, the generations that remember, and the thread of love and wisdom that connects them.

As the storyteller steps back and the echoes of his voice begin to fade, something beautiful remains: the questions that were asked, the laughter that was shared, and the life lessons passed down gently, like heirlooms of the heart.

Writing this book brought me immense joy, but also moments of quiet struggle—especially in harmonizing the vast worlds of a man nearing a century of life and children just beginning to explore theirs. It felt, at times, like composing a melody with notes drawn from different centuries. And yet, that harmony unfolded naturally—through love, patience, and the magic of conversation.

Like all journeys, this one, too, finds its rest. And though it leaves me with a heavy heart, I know it's not truly an end. For as long as these stories are read, as long as even one lesson is carried forward, **Great Grandpa's** voice lives on—gentle, wise, and smiling.

So here we are—on the last page. But not at the end.

With heartfelt gratitude and hope,
M.N. Ashraf

9 789334 376883

Printed at Repro India Ltd.